NCERT
QUESTIONS-ANSWERS

English Core

Textbooks : Hornbill (Prose & Poetry)
& Snapshots (Supplementary Reader)

CLASS
11

NCERT

QUESTIONS-ANSWERS

English Core

Textbooks : Hornbill (Prose & Poetry)
& Snapshots (Supplementary Reader)

CLASS 11

by

Beena Chaturvedi

✱arihant

Arihant Prakashan (School Division Series)

✳arihant
ARIHANT PRAKASHAN MEERUT
All Rights Reserved

꣼ Administrative & Production Offices
Regd. Office
'Ramchhaya' 4577/15, Agarwal Road, Darya Ganj, New Delhi -110002
Tele: 011- 47630600, 43518550

꣼ Head Office
Kalindi, TP Nagar, Meerut (UP) - 250002
Tel: 0121-7156203, 7156204

꣼ Sales & Support Offices
Agra, Ahmedabad, Bengaluru, Bareilly, Chennai, Delhi, Guwahati, Hyderabad, Jaipur, Jhansi, Kolkata, Lucknow, Nagpur & Pune.

꣼ ISBN   978-93-27198-08-9

PO No : TXT-XX-XXXXXXX-X-XX

Published by Arihant Publications (India) Ltd.

For further information about the books published by Arihant, log on to www.arihantbooks.com or e-mail at info@arihantbooks.com

Follow us on 🅕 🅔 ▶ 🅞

Preface

Feeling the immense importance and value of NCERT books, we are presenting this book, having the NCERT Exercises Solutions. For the overall benefit of the students we have made this book unique in such a way that it presents not only solutions but also detailed explanations. Through these detailed and through explanations, students can learn the concepts which will enhance their thinking and learning abilities.

The **Story Retold** At the start of each prose chapter, detailed summary with outlines have been given. By studying it, students can understand the chapter and can make them well-versed with it and will be able to answer all possible questions concerned to a particular chapter whether it is Long Answer Type or Short Answer Type.

Stanzawise Explanation At the start of each poem, detailed explanation of each and every stanza of the poem have been given. By studying it, students can understand the chapter and can make them well-versed with it and will be able to answer all possible questions concerned to a particular chapter whether it is Extract Based Questions or Short Answer Type Questions.

Intext Questions The intext questions given in between the chapters have also been thoroughly dealt with to enhance the critical ability and understanding of the students.

With the hope that this book will be of great help to the students, we wish great success to our readers.

Beena Chaturvedi

Contents

Hornbill-PROSE

Hornbill-POETRY

Snapshots-SUPPLEMENTARY

1

The Portrait of a Lady

Khushwant Singh

Chapter Sketch

The chapter, 'The Portrait of a Lady' by 'Khushwant Singh' is a fond recollection of his grandmother. The author shared a very strong bond with his grandmother. Their relationship underwent several changes but mutual love, respect and understanding were always present.

The Story Retold

The author recollects and describes his grand parents, physical attributes, especially his grandmother's

According to the author, his grandmother, like everybody's grandmother, was an old woman. He could never imagine that once upon a time, she was pretty and had a husband too. The portrait of his grandfather hung on the wall, which showed him wearing a turban and having a white beard. He looked at least a hundred years old. The grandmother was short and fat but her presence in the house always had a soothing and calming influence on the author.

The author stayed with his grandmother in the village and went to school

The author's parents went to the city and left him along with his grandmother in the village. The author enjoyed going to the village school with his grandmother. The grandmother would get him ready and would accompany him to the school. While the author learnt his lessons at school, the grandmother would read scriptures inside the adjoining temple.

The turning point in their life when the author and his grandmother shifted to the city

The author's parents comfortably settled in the city and asked them to come. In the city, the author had to go to an English school by a motor bus and the grandmother could not help him with his lessons because they were in a language, which was beyond grandmother's understanding. There was no outing for grandmother any more. She started feeding the sparrows, like she fed the village dogs.

As the years passed, the relationship between the author and the grandmother became a little distanced

With the passage of time, the author started having less interaction with his grandmother. The lessons taught in the English school were not really understood by the grandmother. Moreover, the grandmother was not happy about certain things not been given importance in the school such as God and scriptures. She got further distressed by the fact that his grandson was taught music which, according to her, was not for gentle folk.

The author went to the university and the common link of friendship with his grandmother snapped

The author went to the university and no longer shared the room with his grandmother. The grandmother passed her time by her wheel spinning and reciting prayers. Earlier, in the village, she used to feed dogs, whereas in the city she fed sparrows. She rarely talked to anyone. The happiest time in her day was the half-hour break, which she took from her wheel in the afternoon to feed the sparrows.

The author went abroad

The author had to go abroad for higher studies. He was sure that when he would come back, he would not find his grandmother alive. When he was leaving, the grandmother did not become sentimental. She came to the station to bid him farewell.

Grandmother still alive when the author returned from abroad and celebrated his home-coming

After five years, the author came back and found his grandmother at the station. She did not look any older. In the evening, something strange happened. The grandmother did not say her prayer. She called neighbourhood women and got an old drum. For several hours, she thumped the drum and sang songs of the home-coming of warriors. The author and his family members tried to stop her to avoid over straining but she did not listen.

The grandmother fell sick and passed away

Next morning, the grandmother got a mild fever. The doctor was not unduly worried but the grandmother insisted that her end was near. She told everyone that she did not want to talk to anyone and would rather spend her last moments praying. She ignored everyone and started telling her beads. After a short while, the author noticed that his grandmother's lips stopped moving. She died a peaceful death.

The sparrows paid their last respect to the grandmother

When the author and others came to take the grandmother's body, they met a strange sight. A lot of sparrows had surrounded the grandmother's body. They were all silent. When the author's mother offered the sparrows some bread, they refused to eat and quietly flew away after the grandmother's body was carried outside.

Exercises

Notice these expressions

Question 1. "the thought was almost revolting"

Answer The thought that the author's grandmother was once young and pretty raises a doubt in the mind of the author. He finds it too hard to believe, as he had always seen her in the same old and wrinkled physical condition for the last twenty years.

Question 2. "an expanse of pure white serenity"

Answer It refers to the calm, peaceful and serene character and conduct of the author's grandmother. She is compared to the peaceful winter landscape in the mountains. She was always attired in spotless white clothes and had silver hair. She, thus, presented a picture of pure white serenity.

Question 3. "a turning-point"

Answer It refers to the point where the author's relationship with his grandmother changes drastically after they move to the city-house. The grandmother is unable to accompany the author to school as he travels by motor bus. Neither is she able to help him in his lessons. Although they share the same room, a sort of distancing occurred in the relationship.

Question 4. "accepted her seclusion with resignation"

Answer This shows the author's grandmother's passive submission to her secluded life after she gradually loses touch with her grandson. When the author was given a room of his own, the common link of friendship between the two was snapped. However, the grandmother accepted her fate without complaint. She rarely talked to anyone in the house and was busy spinning the wheel and reciting her prayers. Even when she relaxed, it was to feed the sparrows.

Question 5. "a veritable bedlam of chirpings"

Answer It refers to the noise, confusion and chaos caused by the chirping of the sparrows that scattered and perched around the author's grandmother. The grandmother sat in the verandah and broke the bread into little bits and threw it to the sparrows. Hundreds of sparrows collected around her and created a noise by their continuous chirping.

Question 6. "frivolous rebukes"

Answer It refers to the casual and light-hearted rebukes of the grandmother to the sparrows. That day she realised that she would die and so was having some fun with the sparrows by scolding them for small mistakes. The grandmother had developed a special bond with the sparrows. The sparrows came in huge numbers and the grandmother fed them with little bits of bread. Sometimes she also used to scold them. The sparrows perched on her legs, shoulders and even sat on her head but she smiled and never shooed them away.

Question 7. "the sagging skins of the dilapidated drum"

Answer It points to the shabby and deteriorated condition of the drum. The grandmother celebrated the homecoming of the author by collecting the women of the neighbourhood and getting an old drum. For several hours, she beat the worn out drum and sang the songs related to the homecoming of warriors.

Understanding the text

Question 1. Mention the three phases of the author's relationship with his grandmother before he left the country to study abroad.

Answer

(i) For the author, Khushwant Singh, his grandmother, like everybody's grandmother, was an old woman who could never be young and pretty but was always beautiful. Her presence always exuded peace and contentment.

(ii) When the auhor's parents went to live in the city and left him with his grandmother, she took utmost care of him right from waking him up in the morning, to getting him ready for the school, taking him to and bringing him back from the school. Both enjoyed an easy companionship.

(iii) The author's parents asked for them to come to the city. This was the time when Khushwant Singh's relationship with his grandmother changed. The author went to a city school and subsequently, to the university, and slowly the friendship between them weakened.

Question 2. Mention three reasons why the author's grandmother was disturbed when he started going to school.

Answer

(i) The lessons taught in the city school were in English and the topics such as little things of Western science, law of gravity etc were all beyond grandmother's comprehension. She could not help her grandson with his lessons so, she was unhappy.

(ii) She had no faith in the things that were taught in the English school and was distressed that there was no teaching about God and scriptures.

(iii) She was very unhappy when she came to know that music lessons were taught in her grandson's school. She always associated music with harlots and beggars and not with gentle folk.

Question 3. Mention three ways in which the author's grandmother spent her days after he grew up.

Answer

(i) The author's grandmother rarely left her spinning wheel. From sunrise to sunset, she sat by her spinning wheel.

(ii) While she sat by her spinning wheel, she recited her prayers and did not talk to anyone.

(iii) In the afternoon, she relaxed for a while to feed the sparrows. While she sat on the verandah breaking the bread into little bits, hundreds of little birds collected surrounding her.

Question 4. Mention the odd way in which the author's grandmother behaved just before she died.

Answer   Just before the day the grandmother died, a change came upon her. She did not pray in the evening. She got an old drum and started singing for her grandson, which went on for hours. Next morning, she was taken ill. The doctor thought nothing of it but the grandmother thought differently.

She told everyone that her end was near and since her end was near, she would spend last of her living moments in prayer and would not waste her time in talking to anyone. She lay peacefully in bed praying and before anyone could suspect, her lips stopped moving. She passed away peacefully.

Question 5. Mention the way in which the sparrows expressed their sorrow when the author's grandmother died.

Answer In the evening, when the author and his family members went where grandmother's body was lying, they saw thousands of sparrows sitting scattered on the floor. There was no chirruping. The author's mother offered some bread to them, but the sparrows took no notice. After the grandmother's corpse was taken, the sparrows flew away quietly.

Talking about the text

Question 1. The author's grandmother was a religious person. What are the different ways in which we come to know this?

Answer Following are the ways in which we come to know that the author's grandmother was a religious person
  (i) She hobbled about the house in a white saree, always carrying and telling the beads of her rosary.
 (ii) When the author was in the village with her, he would always find her saying morning prayer while she bathed and dressed him up.
(iii) The grandmother would always go to the village school with her grandson because the school was attached to the temple. While the children were taught, the grandmother would sit inside the temple and read scriptures.
(iv) She would always feed the animals (dogs in the village) and birds (sparrows in the city) because she thought it to be a part of religious rituals.
 (v) The last moments of her life were spent in praying rather than talking to her family members.

Question 2. Describe the changing relationship between the author and his grandmother. Did their feeling for each other change?

Answer The author and his grandmother shared a relationship which was very strong. The author had a lot of respect and admiration for his grandmother and her love for the author was limitless. Earlier, they shared everything including the room. This closeness strengthened their bond. When the author was asked to shift to the city along with his grandmother to stay with his parents, their relationship underwent a change.

Their interaction became less as the author grew older. He moved to a foreign university for five years. Even though now the physical proximity was less, conversation lesser, but the basic foundation of their relationship was extremely strong. The grandmother kept a tenacious hold on to her life till her grandson returned from abroad. Only after seeing him, she breathed her last.

Question 3. Would you agree that the author's grandmother was a strong person in character? If yes, give instances that show this.

Answer The author's grandmother, indeed, was a strong person in character. The following instances can reinstate the above statement

(i) The author compares his grandmother to the 'winter landscape in the mountains', which breathes peace and contentment. Only a strong person exudes peace and comfort.

(ii) The grandmother took absolute care of her grandson when he was left in her custody in the village. She took all the pains to give good education to him and instill values in him.

(iii) When she realised that she was no longer required to assist her grandson, she accepted her 'seclusion' with resignation and learnt to pass her time in a way she liked the most. She did not impose herself on anyone.

(iv) The author, while leaving abroad for further studies, thought that on his return, the grandmother would not be alive as she was very old. But, he undermined his grandmother's resilience and strong will. Though she became very frail, she waited for her grandson to come back. After five years, the author returned. The grandmother celebrated his home-coming and next day passed away peacefully.

Question 4. Have you known someone like the author's grandmother? Do you feel the same sense of loss with regard to someone whom you have loved and lost?

Answer My own grandfather was exactly like author's grandmother.

I always used to search for words that could describe my grandfather and when I read "like the winter landscape in the mountains, an expanse of pure white serenity breathing peace and contentment", it seemed that the author had given words to my imagination for my grandfather's description.

He was an epitome of patience, fortitude and courage. He was a source of inspiration not only to me but a host of others as well. He also died at a ripe age just like author's grandmother. But there are some people whose loss is irreparable. Th void left after my grandfather's death can never be filled.

Thinking about language

Question 1. Which language do you think the author and his grandmother used while talking to each other?

Answer The author and his grandmother used to live in a village and belonged to a Punjabi Sikh family. Therefore, they must have used their mother tongue, Punjabi, to converse with each other.

Working with words

Question 1. Notice the following uses of the word 'tell'. Match the meanings to the uses listed below.

Answer
1. Her fingers were busy *telling* the beads of her rosary. [count while reciting]
2. I would *tell* her English words and little things of Western science and learning. [make something known to someone in spoken or written form]
3. At her age, one could never *tell*. [be sure]
4. She *told* us that her end was near. [give information to somebody]

Question 2. Notice the different senses of the word 'take'.
1. to take something : to begin to do something as a habit.
2. to take ill : to suddenly become ill.

Locate these phrases in the text and notice the way they are used.

Answer
1. She took to feeding sparrows in the courtyard of our city house. Earlier she used to feel the dogs in the village and now she started feeding the sparrows in the city.

2. The next morning she was taken ill. The previous evening, she sang songs for several hours and the next morning, she suddenly became sick.

Question 3. The word 'hobble' means to walk with difficulty because the legs and feet are in bad condition.

Tick the words in the box below that also refer to a manner of walking.

Haggle, Shuffle, Stride, Ride, Waddle, Wriggle, Paddle, Swagger, Trudge, Slog

Answer These words are: Shuffule, stride, waddle, paddle, swagger, trudge, slog.

Things to do

Question 1. Talk with your family members about elderly people who have been intimately connected with and who are not there with you now. Write a short description of someone you liked a lot.

Note *I have written this answer as a long answer which is a pattern of the question papers. Word limit 150 words.*

Answer Short Description of Someone You Liked a Lot

It is very ironic that we realise the importance of a person when he/she is not around. My grandfather was an idol not only for me but for a lot of other people also. Travelling down the memory lane, I am not able to find any corner of my life in which his presence goes unnoticed.

From the very beginning, my grandfather insisted only on one thing : Be honest to yourself. Do not be indifferent towards others. Always be assertive about your convictions and beliefs.

He had seen many ups and downs in life, but never lost his balance. He had the ability to adapt himself to any situation, good or bad. He extended a helping hand to one and all who wanted it.

His demise was not unexpected but when it happened, I felt as if I was struck by a thunderbolt. I cherish all that he has given to me and I am sure I will be able to face life with courage and strength.

2

"We're Not Afraid to Die... If We Can All Be Together"

Gordon Cook and Alan East

Chapter Sketch

The story is about a family, which undertakes a sea voyage in their boat 'Wavewalker'. They encounter a lot of problems on their way. It is their indomitable courage, strength and the feeling of togetherness that helps them keep their wits together and over come all the odds.

"We're not afraid to die ... if we can all be together."

The Story Retold

The voyage begins

The author and his wife, Mary, alongwith their two children, Jonathan and Suzanne, started their sea voyage in their boat 'Wave walker' on 7th July.

When they reached Cape Town, the author, from plymouth, was also the captain of the voyage, took two crewman-American Larry Vigil and Swiss Herb Seigler. They were about to sail into one of the world's roughest seas, the southern Indian Ocean.

Encountering dangers of the sea

On the second day out of Cape-town, they encountered strong winds and high waves. Inspite of the atrocious weather, they celebrated Christmas with a lot of fun. The weather did not change even with the advent of New Year.

The captain meets; with an accident and almost dies

On 2nd January, the waves were really high. The ship was tossing around with the waves. The captain and his crew tried their level best to minimise the damage. They tied heavy mooring ropes at the back end of the boat, dropped the storm jib, put on their life jackets and attached lifelines. At about 6 pm, there was an ominous silence, followed by a huge thunder. A gigantic wave appeared and there was an explosion. Water broke over the ship and the captain was thrown into sea. He thought that his end is approaching.

As the injured captain resigned to his fate, he saw his boat nearly sinking. Suddenly a wave hurled him upright, which tightened the captain's lifeline. He got tossed on the deck of the boat by the waves. He found the wheel and lined up the stern. His crewman pumped the water out like mad. The captain managed to find some tools, screws and canvas, and covered the leaking holes. When he had problems with hand pumps, he managed to get an electric pump to drain out the water.

The captain's daughter's injury

The captain and his crew worked endlessly, pumping the water out to keep the ship afloat. His daughter, Sue, got an injury on her head, and arm which was bad. However, she behaved like a brave girl and thought nothing about it.

No change on January 3 and 4

On 3rd January, the water level was under control but there, still, was a big leak somewhere. The ship was in a bad condition. They could not have reached Australia. Their only hope was to reach a nearby, small island Ile Amsterdam. On 4th January, they had to keep pace with the water still coming in. They had their first meal in two days.

The captain's family's optimism

On 4th January, at about 4 pm, black clouds gathered up, the wind started blowing and the waves rode higher. The captain went to his children to comfort them but they turned out to be brave and optimistic. His son told him that he was not afraid to die as long as all of them were together. This optimism gave the captain more strength to fight the situation. On 6th January, the weather improved. He tried to work on wind speed. His daughter tried to inspire him by giving him a beautiful 'Best of Luck' card.

Ile Amsterdam sighted

The captain asked Larry to steer a course of 185 degree, which may bring them to Ile Amsterdam. The captain did not feel very hopeful and dozed off. At about 6 pm, his children woke him up and told him that he was the best father and the best captain in the whole world because he had found the island.

The indomitable spirit of Wavewalker's occupants

The captain, Larry, Herbie, Mary, Sue and Jon-all proved that grit and optimism can defeat even the direst circumstances.

We're not afraid to die ... if we can all be together.

Exercises

Notice these expressions

Notice these expressions in the text. Infer their meaning from the context.

Question 1. "honing our seafaring skills"

Answer   It refers to the efforts made by the narrator and his wife to perfect and sharpen their knowledge of navigation, handling of the boat and equipment and other sea skills.

Question 2. "ominous silence"

Answer   It refers to the silence just before an impending danger. The peace and quiet suggests that something bad is going to happen.

Question 3. "Mayday calls"

Answer   They are radio-telephonic calls which are given by aircraft or ships stuck in a disastrous situation. They are distress calls made to secure help from other ships nearby.

Question 4. "pinpricks in the vast ocean"

Answer   This phrase refers to tiny islands in a vast ocean. They are so small that they appear like tiny pinheads on a map of the vast ocean.

Question 5. "a tousled head"

Answer   It refers to hair in disarray or the disarranged hair of the author's son. His hair was all messed up and uncombed.

Understanding the text

Question 1. List the steps taken by the captain.

(i) To protect the ship when rough weather began.

Answer To protect the ship when rough weather began, the captain took the following steps

(a) To slow the boat down, the captain dropped the storm jib and lashed a heavy mooring rope in a loop across the stern.

(b) He then double lashed everything, and went through the life raft drill.

(c) The captain then attached lifelines, donned oilskins and life jackets.

(ii) To check the flooding of the water in the ship.

Answer To check the flooding of the water in the ship, the following steps were taken

(a) The captain stretched canvas and secured waterproof hatch covers across the gaping holes. With this step taken, the water still seeped, but most of it was now being deflected over the side.

(b) When the hand pumps started to block up, the author found another electric pump under the chartroom floor and connected it to an out pipe.

Question 2. Describe the mental condition of the voyagers on 4th and 5th January.

Answer On 4th January, the mental condition of the voyagers was vascillating between hope and despair. After 36 hours of continuous pumping, water had receded but they still had to keep pace with the water still coming in. The captain's wife provided them with the first meal in two days of some corned beef and cracker biscuits. However, this respite was only short-lived. The storm started building up and the situation again became worse.

On 5th January, the situation was desperate. When the captain went to his children to comfort them, the small boy asked him innocently if they all were going to die but added that he did not mind dying as long as all were the family members were together. This strengthened the captain's determination to fight all odds and survive.

Question 3. Describe the shifts in the narration of the events as indicated in the three sections of the text. Give a subtitle to each section.

Answer Subtitle The Hazardous sea-voyage, the first section of the narration narrates the enthusiastic preparations and the sea voyage, which the captain, along with his family members, undertook in July, 1976. Their boat 'wave walker' was a professionally built boat, which completed the first leg of their planned three-year journey pleasantly. At this point of their journey, the captain took on two crewman– American Larry Vigil and Swiss Herb Seigler to help them tackle one of the world's roughest seas - the southern Indian ocean.

In the first section, we notice a shift in the narration when the captain and his crew encountered atrocious weather. The high sea waves were creating havoc. The boat started leaking. There was water everywhere and to make it more worse, the captain met with an accident.

There were some other mishaps also with the other family members. The good part was that all those who started the voyage were still together.

Facing Tough Situations with Grit and Determination

The second part of the narration deals with the efforts put in to over come the ordeal. It also shows the brighter side of human nature. The captain and his family members showed exemplary courage and strength in the face of disaster. This section cleary gives a very meaningful lesson 'United we stand'. Even the young ones in the family displayed how a positive lookout can help in overcoming the greatest difficulties. One should never bow down and meekly accept the problem.

Perseverance and Optimism Lead to Victory

The third part of the narration sees the 'wavewalker' and its occupants reach the island Ile-Amsterdam. Initially, the captain had lost hope that they could reach the island. Suddenly, a cheerful announcement by his son that he was the best father and the best captain made him realise that after all, they had reached the island. It seemed the most beautiful island in the world even though it was only a bleak piece of volcanic rock with a little vegetation.

Talking about the text

Question 1. Discuss the following questions with your partner.

What difference did you notice between the reaction of the children and the adults when faced with danger?

Answer There was not much of a difference between the reaction of the children and the adults when faced with danger. Both showed courage and strength. The children showed a more positive frame of mind. The captain and his crew members tried to save the boat but the impetus given to the captain was from his son who said that he was not afraid to die as long as they were together.

Question 2. How does the story suggest that optimism helps to endure 'the direst stress'?

Answer The story runs between hope and despair. The sea-voyage started on a note of hope and enthusiasm, and ended on a note of fulfillment. During the voyage, the boat had to sail in rough waters. The captain managed to steer the boat to an island. At times, his failing courage got the boost from his family members and crew. His wife stayed at the wheels in the crucial hours, his seven years old girl did not let them worry about her head injury and his six years old boy was not afraid to die.

Question 3. What lessons do we learn from such hazardous experiences when we are face to face with death?

Answer The most important lesson that we learn from such hazardous experiences, when we are face-to-face with death, is not to lose hope under any circumstances. At times, life presents very dire situations but if one is optimistic about finding a solution and overcomes the odds, one will always be successful.

Question 4. Why do you think people undertake such adventurous expedition in spite of the risks involved?

Answer Most of us like to lead a risk free life but there are a few of us who believe that if we want to live life to the fullest, we have to go beyond day-to-day routine. If that was not the case, a lot of mysteries, places and events would not have been known to the world. The urge to do something out of the ordinary forces people to take adventurous expeditions, inspite of the risks involved.

Thinking about language

Question 1. We have come across words like 'gale' and 'storm' in the account. Here are two more words for 'storm': typhoon, cyclone. How many words does your language have for 'storm'?

Answer In Hindi, 'storm' is known as 'aandhi', 'toofan', 'jhanjavat' and 'chakravat'.

Question 2. Here are the terms for different kinds of vessels: yatch, boat, canoe, ship, steamer, schooner. Think of similar terms in your language.

Answer 'Naav', 'Nauka', 'Pot', 'Jahaaz' and 'Kishti' are some of the words used in Hindi for the word 'boat'.

Question 3. 'Catamaran' is a kind of a boat. Do you know which Indian language this word is derived from? Check the dictionary.

Answer The word 'Catamaran' is derived from the Tamil word 'Kattumaram', that means 'tied wood'.

Catamaran is a name applied to any craft having twin hulls. Originally, it denoted a form of sailing and paddling raft employed on the coasts of India.

Question 4. Have you heard any boatmen's songs? What kind of emotions do these songs usually express?

Answer Yes, I have heard boatmen's songs. They usually express love and nostalgia. Boatmen sing these songs to curb their longing and express their love.

Working with words

Question 1. The following words used in the text as ship terminology are also commonly used in another sense. In what contexts would you use the other meaning?

> Knot, Stern, Boom, Hatch, Anchor

Answer
- (a) **Knot**   A fastening
  - The villagers tied the culprit in a secured knot.
- (b) **Stern**   Serious, disapproving
  - The teacher's stern look silenced the wrong doer.
- (c) **Boom**   A loud deep sound
  - The chaos turned into order the moment the leader addressed the public with a boom in his voice.
- (d) **Hatch**
  - (i) Young ones of a bird, fish or reptile comes out of the egg.
    - It is strange that crows hatch the bird Koel's eggs.
  - (ii) To form a plot or plan.
    - The terrorists were nabbed by the police before they could hatch another attack.
- (e) **Anchor** A person who presents a live television or radio programme.
  - Harsha Bhogal is the best sports anchor in the present time.

Question 2. The following three compound words end in ship. What does each of them mean? Airship, Flagship, Lightship

Answer

- (a) **Airship**   A large power driven aircraft filled with a gas which is lighter than air.
- (b) **Flagship**   The ship in a fleet which carries the commanding officer.
- (c) **Lightship** A ship with lights to guide other ships.

Question 3. The following are the meanings listed in the dictionary against the phrase 'take on'. In which meaning is it used in the third paragraph of the account?

Answer   In the third paragraph of the account, the phrase 'take on' is used as 'to employ', 'to engage'.

Before heading East, we 'took on' two crewmen - American Larry Vigil and Swiss Herb Seigler.

3

Discovering Tut :
The Saga Continues

A R Williams

Chapter Sketch

The lesson deals with the attempts to find about King Tut, the last ruler of a very powerful dynasty in Egypt, who died at a very young age of 18 years. Since the discovery of his tomb in 1922, the entire world wanted to know about this young King's life and his death.

The Story Retold

King Tut's mummy was taken for a CT Scan after 80 years of its discovery

On 5th January, 2005, the world's most famous mummy was taken for a CT Scan. King Tut was the last heir of a very powerful family in Egypt, who had ruled for centuries. Since the discovery of his tomb in 1922, the whole world has been curious to find about him and his death.

Howard Carter and his findings

Howard Carter was a British archaeologist, who in 1922, discovered King Tut's tomb. What he found in the tomb was the richest royal collection, which caused a sensation. Carter also found that Tut was buried with everday things like board games, a bronze razor, cases of food and wine alongwith stunning artefacts in gold.

Carter's investigation of three nested coffins and the trouble he ran into

Carter found Tut's body in three nested coffins. In the first coffin, Carter found a shroud, which was decorated with garlands of willow and olive leaves, lotus petals and cornflowers. When he finally reached the mummy, he found the resins, which were a part of the ritual, had hardened, cementing Tut to the bottom of his solid gold coffin.

Carter's cutting the mummy and his defense

To find more about King Tut's life and death, his remains had to be examined. However, because of hardened resins, Carter had to chisel away from beneath the limbs and trunk of Tut's mummy. He defended this by saying that if he hadn't cut the mummy, thieves certainly would have stolen all the valuables, which were buried alongwith Tut's body.

Tut's mummy X-rayed and some startling facts revealed

In 1968, more than 40 years after Carter's discovery, an anatomy professor X-rayed Tut's mummy and revealed a startling fact that beneath the resins that caked Tut's chest, his breast bone and front ribs were missing.

King Tut and his ancestors

King Tut's father or grandfather-Amenhotep-III was a powerful king, who ruled for almost four decades. His son Amenhotep IV succeeded him. He was a very strange king. He changed his name to Akhenaten and moved the religious capital from Thebes to Akhetaten. He attacked a major God 'Amun' by smashing his images and closing down his temples. Ray Johnson, director of the University of Chicago's research center, called this king wacky. After Akhenaten, Smenkhkare ruled for a brief period and then young King Tut took over the throne. He oversaw restoration of old ways. King Tut ruled for nine years and then died unexpectedly.

King Tut's mummy and CT Scan

No one knows how many mummies there are in Egypt. Egyptian Mummy Project has recorded almost six hundred and is still counting. King Tut's mummy was the first mummy to be CT scanned by a portable scanner donated by National Geographic Society and Siemens.

Tut's mummy was scanned from head to toe

Tut's entire body was scanned. On the night of the scan, workmen carried him from the tomb and rose on a hydraulic lift into a trailer that held the scan. There were problems. The costly scanner could not function properly because of sand in the cooler fan. But all the hurdles were crossed and after the scan, the king returned to his coffin to rest in peace.

The findings of CT Scan as scientist heaved a sigh of relief

The CT Scan showed an astonishing image of Tut and his entire body, very clearly. Zahi Hawass, secretary General of Egypt's supreme council of antiques, was relieved that nothing, had seriously gone wrong. As the technicians left the trailer, they saw the star constellation which ancient Egyptians, called the 'God of afterlife'. They felt as if the God was watching over the boy king.

Exercises

Notice these expressions

Question 1. "forensic reconstruction"

Answer It refers to rebuilding the facts about life and death by putting back together the evidence to examine a crime scientifically. The reconstruction of King Tut's mummy was done to find solutions to the mysteries surrounding his death.

Question 2. "funerary treasures"

Answer It refers to the valuables and treasures which were buried along with the pharaoh in the pyramid.

Question 3. "scudded across"

Answer It refers to moving swiftly from one place to another. It is used in the chapter to describe the movement of the dark-bellied clouds.

Question 4. "casket grey"

Answer It refers to ash coloured clouds that hid the stars.

Question 5. "resurrection"

Answer It refers to rebirth or revival after death.

Question 6. "circumvented"

Answer Outsmarted or outwitted. The thieves would have easily bypassed the guards with artfulness and ripped the mummy apart to remove the gold.

Question 7. "computed tomography"

Answer It refers to CT scan that provides the X-ray image of a body in cross section. It is used for diagnostic purposes.

Question 8. "eerie detail"

Answer It refers to detail relating to the supernatural.

Understanding the text

Question 1. Give reasons for the following

(i) King Tut's body has been subjected to repeated scrutiny.

Answer King Tut's body has been subjected to repeated scrutiny because right from the time of the discovery of his tomb in 1922, the modern world has been curious to find out what happened to him, with murder being the most extreme possibility.

(ii) Howard Carter's investigation was resented.

Answer Howard Carter's investigation was resented because Carter's men removed the mummy's head and severed nearly every major joint of the body to raise Tut's body from the coffin.

(iii) Carter had to chisel away the solidified resins to raise the King's remains.

Answer Carter had to chisel away the solidified resins to raise the King's remains because the ritual resins had hardened, cementing Tut to the bottom of his solid gold coffin, which no amount of legitimate force could move.

(iv) Tut's body was buried alongwith gilded treasures.

Answer Tut's body was buried alongwith gilded treasures because in that time, the royals were fabulously wealthy and they thought and hoped that they could take their riches with them in their journey to the great beyond.

(v) **The boy changed his name from Tutan khaten to Tutan khamun.**

Answer The boy changed his name from Tutan khaten to Tutan khamun because he wanted the restoration of the old ways. His ancestor had shocked the country by attacking 'Amun', a major God, and it was a shocking time. Tutan khamun means 'living image of Amun'.

Question 2. (i) **List the deeds that led Ray Johnson to describe Akhenaten as 'whacky'.**

Answer Ray Johnson described Akhenaten as 'whacky' for the his following deeds

(a) Akhenaten first changed his name and moved the religious capital from the old city of Thebes to the new city of Akhenaten.

(b) He further shocked the country by attacking 'Amun' a major God, by smashing his images and closing his temples.

(ii) **What were the results of the CT Scan?**

Answer The CT Scan showed King Tut's neck vertebrae, a hand and several views of the rib-cage and a transection of the skull. All of it showed that nothing had gone seriously wrong.

(iii) **List the advances in technology that have improved forensic analysis.**

Answer The advances in technology that have improved forensic analysis are as follows

1. Today, diagonistic imaging can be done by computed tomography or CT.

2. In CT, hundreds of X-rays in cross-section are put together like slices of bread to create a three dimensional virtual body.

3. The X-ray images in cross section can scan even the intricate structure by reducing it to slices in millimetres.

(iv) **Explain the statement, "King Tut is one of the first mummy to be scanned in death as in life."**

Answer King Tut was the last heir of a powerful family that had ruled Egypt for centuries. He met a very early death just when he was 18 years old. Since the discovery of his tomb in 1922, the world has speculated a lot about him. Tut's mummy had to undergo a CT Scan that offered new clues about his life and death. His mummy was the first to go for a CT scan, hence, in death as in life, he moved regally ahead of his countrymen.

Talking about the text

Discuss the following

Question 1. Scientific invention is necessary to unearth buried mysteries.

Answer A man has to learn a lot of things from his past to face the present for a bright future. One can never learn only from imagination. We need to have solid, concerete proof in front of us to enhance our knowledge. *E.g.,* if King Tut's mummy was not subjected to scientific scrutiny, we would never have known more about the great and the last heir of a powerful family that had ruled Egypt for centuries.

There is certainly a need to use scientific invention to find what happened to someone, centuries ago. If we want to know what happened long time back, we can read about it in History. The scientific, scrutiny of King Tut's mummy helped the modern world to discover a lot of things about the king that would, otherwise, have remained unknown. King Tut was the last heir of a powerful family who died young. Whether he has murdered or died a natural death is a matter of interest to archaeologists.

Question 2. Advanced technology gives us conclusive evidence of past events.

Answer In Favour Science is known for its precision. If any thing is subjected To analysis to come to a definite conclusion, advanced technology indeed helps. *E.g.,* CT Scan of King Tut's mummy has offered new clues about his life and death, and provides precise data for accurate forensic reconstruction of the young king. It helped to probe the lingering medical mysteries of the young ruler, who died more than 3,300 years ago.

Against No doubt, advanced technology helps but what is beyond comprehension that should be used to find conclusive evidence of the past when the present itself is laden with so many mysteries. Even the advanced technology can not always be correct.

Question 3. Traditions, rituals and funerary practice must be respected.

Answer In Favour Any society can progress only if it does not let go its roots. We may ridicule certain traditions, scoff at rituals and mock at funerary practice. But, all these old practices have certain mythological values attached to them. There is a belief, not only in India but outside also, that the death is only an end to the physical being. The soul has to travel further. King Tut was buried with everyday things he may want in the afterlife such as board games, bronze razor, cases of food and wine.

Against   Human beings are known for their discretionary power. Traditions, rituals and funerary practices should be given due respect but we should understand one thing very clearly. The practice which carries no meaning should be discarded. The dead body should be cremated with honour but burying it with everyday things has no relevance. Why would a dead person need food, water and razors? We should learn to respect and not to follow blind foldedly.

Question 4. Knowledge about the past is useful to complete our knowledge of the world we live in.

Answer   In Favour   Our past is our best teacher. From our past experiences, We learn not to commit the same mistakes, which resulted in disaster. The knowledge of our past helps us to understand about the ideas, which can be understood and followed to pave our way to success. The revelation of King Tut's mummy helped to understand the ancient culture of Egypt, which brought us a clear understanding of the gradual changes in the culture of that country.

Against Knowledge of the past, no doubt, is useful to understand and make our present more productive. But the world is changing at a rapid speed. For us, even what had happened an hour earlier, may not have significance for tomorrow. Everyday, new inventions are taking place, new discoveries are made. So, knowledge about the past may be useful but not always essential.

Thinking about language

Read the following piece of information from the Encyclopaedia of Language by David Crystal.

Egyptian is now extinct: its history dates from before the third millennium BC, preserved in many hieroglyphic inscriptions and papyrus manuscripts. Around the second century AD, it developed into a language known as Coptic. Coptic may still have been used as late as the early nineteenth century and is still used as a religious language by Monophysite Christians in Egypt.

Question 1.   What do you think are the reasons for the extinction of languages?

Answer   Some of the reasons for the extinction of languages are
  (a) Migration of people to other lands.
  (b) Limitation of vocabulary.
  (c) Absence of written script along with prevalence of oral tradition.
  (d) Globalisation, as it has led to the use of only dominant languages.

(e) Social status of a language.

(f) Introduction of a non-indigeneous language that takes over all social functions.

(g) Constant changes in the society.

(h) Parents do not pass on a language to their children.

Question 2. Do you think it is important to preserve languages?

Answer Yes, it is important to preserve languages as they are responsible for development of the culture of the community. It helps in preservation of one's heritage and traditions. Our language defines our identity. One can differentiate between the people speaking the same language by their dialect or the way they talk. A language represents a whole cultural history. 'Linguistic diversity' is a benchmark of cultural diversity. Language is a cultural resource and it should be handed down by parents to their children.

Question 3. In what ways do you think we could help prevent the extinction of languages and dialects?

Answer We could help prevent the extinction of languages and dialects by

(a) Transferring the vocabulary and dialects of the language to the next generation.

(b) Documenting the language and preserving information about native literature and linguistics of the language.

(c) Encouraging younger generations to speak the language as they grow.

(d) New technologies such as 'podcasts' can be used to preserve the spoken versions of languages.

(e) Teaching the languages in college and universities and encouraging students to specialise in the same.

Working with words

Question 5. Given below are some interesting combination of words. Explain why they have been used together?

(a) ghostly dust devils   (b) desert sky

(c) stunning artefacts   (d) funerary treasures

(e) scientific detachment   (f) dark-bellied clouds

(g) casket grey   (h) eternal brilliance

(i) ritual resins   (j) virtual body

Answer

(a) **ghostly dust devils** As King Tut's body was taken from his resting place a strong wind blew that threw away a lot of dust. The dead is always associated with ghost. The noisy dusty wind was giving the impression of devils getting angry by being disturbed.

(b) **desert sky** The sky, which was cloudless, an absolutely clear sky.

(c) **stunning artefacts** Very precious and valuable artefacts that by its looks can leave people speechless.

(d) **funerary treasures** The valuable and precious things which were buried along with King Tut's body.

(e) **scientific detachment** To find the truth, Carter had to chisel away the solidified matter beneath the limbs to raise the remains of King Tut. The emotions did not play any role.

(f) **dark bellied clouds** The huge dark clouds probably containing a lot of rains.

(g) **casket grey** Grey colour is associated with grief. Casket carries the dead bodies. Death brings grief.

(h) **eternal brilliance** The shine that is everlasting. Even the passage of time could not affect their brilliance.

(i) **ritual resins** Resins are dry fruits. But in ancient Egypt, they were used to cover the chest of the dead body before burial, which was a part of the rituals.

(j) **virtual body** A body, that may not really exist but impresses its presence in the mind.

Question 2. Here are some commonly used medical terms. Find out their meanings.

CT	scan	MRI tomography
autopsy	dialysis	ECG
post mortem	angiography	biopsy

Answer CT Scan A CT scan makes use of computer-processed combinations of many X-ray images taken from different angles to produce cross-sectional (tomography) images (virtual 'slices') of specific areas of a scanned object, allowing the user to see inside the object without cutting.

MRI Magnetic Resonance Imaging (MRI) is a diagnostic technique that uses magnetic fields and radio waves to produce a detailed image of the body's soft tissue and bones.

Tomography A method of producing a three - dimensional image of the internal structures of a solid object (like the human body) by the observation and recording of the differences in the effects on the passage of waves of energy hitting those structures.

Autopsy An examination of a body after death to determine the cause of death or the character and extent of changes produced by disease.

Dialysis The purification of blood by separating the waste products from it to replace the normal function of kidneys.

ECG An electrocardiogram (EKG or ECG) is a test that checks for problems with the electrical activity of the heart. It shows the heart's electrical activity as line tracings on paper.

Post mortem (also called post mortem examination) An examination of a dead body to determine the cause of death.

Angiography A procedure performed to view blood vessels after injecting them with a dye that outlines them on an X-ray. This technique can be used to look at arteries in many areas of the body, including the brain, neck (carotids), heart, chest, pulmonary circuit, kidneys, gastrointestinal area and limbs.

Biopsy A medical procedure during which a small sample of tissue is removed from a part of a body. The sample of tissue is then examined under the microscope to look for abnormal cells.

Things to do

Question 1. The constellation Orion is associated with the legend of Osiris, the god of the afterlife. Find out the astronomical descriptions and legends associated with the following.

(i) Ursa Major (Saptarishi mandala)

(ii) Polaris (Dhruva tara)   (iii) Pegasus (Winged horse)

(iv) Sirius (Dog star)   (v) Gemini (Mithuna)

Answer

   (i) **Ursa Major** (*Saptarishi mandala*) Ursa Major is a constellation visible throughout the year in the Northern Hemisphere. It consists of seven stars which form the well-known Big-Dipper. Its name means Great Bear in Latin, and is associated with the Legend of Callisto.

      According to Sanskrit mythology, this group of seven sages (Saptarishi) also moves around the constant star Dhruva tara known as Polaris.

  (ii) **Polaris** (*Dhruva tara*) This star remains constant and always points to the North.

The direction of Ursa Major keeps changing with the passage of the night, but Polaris remains unchanged. It is associated with the legend of Dhruva, a six year old boy who was blessed by Lord Vishnu with a permanent and constant abode in the universe.

(iii) **Pegasus** (*Winged horse*) This is associated with Greek mythology as the winged horse sprung from Medusa's blood. It carries lightning bolts for Zeus. Pegasus' constellation may be seen when the stars are clearly visible.

(iv) **Sirius** (*Dog star*) This is associated with the legend of Orion. It is called 'Dog star' as it represents Orion's large hunting dog. The first glimpse of Sirius at dawn announced the rising of the Nile in ancient Egypt.

(v) **Gemini** (*Mithuna*) A combination of two Nakshatras — Aardhara and Punarvasu and having contradictory qualities.

Question 2. Some of the leaves and flowers mentions in the passage for adorning the dead are willow, olive, celery, lotus cornflower. Which of these are common in our country?

Answer   Willow, olive, lotus and cornflower are common in our country.

Question 3. Name some leaves and flowers that are used as adornments in our country.

Answer   Roses, lotus, mehendi, marigolds, champa and chameli flowers and the leaves of mango, peepal, banana and tulsi are used as adornments in our country.

4

Landscape of the Soul

Nathalie Trouveroy

Chapter Sketch

The lesson explains the different views of western art and asian art. The old tale tells that the art in Asia depicts the inner soul whereas the western art believes in illusionistic likeness. Former is subjective, while the latter is objective. In the lesson, the last section deals with 'outsider art', 'art brut' or 'raw art'. The basic concept of this form of art is that anyone, who has artistic insight can be an artist.

The Story Retold

An old Chinese tale about the painter Wu Daozi

In the 18th century, the painter Wu Daozi was asked by the Chinese emperor Xuanzong to decorate the wall of the palace. When the work was completed, he only wanted the emperor to see it. The painting included forests, mountains, waterfalls and a cave. As the emperor admired the painting, the artist clapped his hands, the door of the cave opened, the artist walked in, never to be seen again. Even the painting vanished.

Contrast presented in another story

There is another story about a Chinese painter, who would not draw the eye of a dragon because he was afraid that he would fly out of the painting. Such stories were part of China's classical education.

The two different forms of art

In 15th century, there was a blacksmith who fell in love with the painter's daughter. The painter was not willing to accept him as son-in-law. The blacksmith sneaked into the painter's studio quietly and painted a fly. It was so life-like that the painter wanted to swat it away. Painter got impressed with the blacksmith and kept him as an apprentice. He also married off his daughter to the blacksmith. Later on, the blacksmith became one of the most famous painters of his age. These stories illustrate that in Europe, art tries to achieve a perfect likeness whereas in Asia, art depicts inner spirit and soul.

The meaning inferred by the Chinese story

The Chinese emperor might have been the ruler of the dynasty but the artist knew the true meaning of his work. The emperor had commissioned the painting but the mysterious works of the universe are only known to the artist.

Different view points of Chinese and Western arts

A European painter wants the viewer to see the painting exactly the same way as he sees it. A Chinese painter does not choose a single view point. He has only created a path for the viewers to see the painting. They can see it from any angle they want to. He does not want to impress the viewer from his view point. This kind of an art needs a participation both at the mental as well as the physical level. This is called conceptual landscape.

Shanshui; conceptual landscape

The literal meaning of Shanshui is 'mountain water', which represents the word 'landscape'. Basically, this represents Daoist view of the universe. The mountain is 'Yang' while the water is 'Yin'. Yang is masculine; Yin is feminine. When there is an interaction between 'Yang' and 'Yin', great works are produced. There is a third element also, a middle void where the interaction takes place. It can be compared to Pranayam-breathe in, retain, breathe out. This middle void in Chinese is represented by unpainted space in white.

Man; the eye of the landscape

Man is the receiver of the communication between these poles of the universe. His presence is essential and that is the reason that he is the 'eye of the landscape'.

Getting inside 'outside art'

Art brut

The concept of art-brut was first propounded by the French painter Jean Dubuffet in 1940s. It was a small movement, which slowly gained momentum. It came to be known as 'outsider art'. This form of art is described as the art of those people who have no formal training in art but have talent and artistic insight.

Rock Garden at Chandigarh

When Dubuffet was mooting his concept in France, an untutored genius in India was creating paradise. He started clearing away a little patch of jungle years back, to create a garden for himself where he could sculpt with stone and recycled material. Today, it is known as Rock Garden at Chandigarh.

India's biggest contributor to outsider art

Rock garden's 80 years old creator director Nek Chand is India's biggest contributor to outsider art. A UK based art magazine 'Raw Vision', in their fifteenth issue, had Nek Chand and his Rock Garden sculpture-women by the waterfall on its front cover.

Recognition of Nek Chand's work

Nek Chand, by his creation, has proved that anything and everything could be material for a work of art. Recognising his contribution, the Swiss Commission for UNESCO has honoured him. A five-month show Realm of Nek Chand was held in leading museums in Switzerland, Belgium, France and Italy. According to Nek Chand, the biggest reward for him was people walking in his garden and enjoying his creations.

Exercises

Notice these expressions

Question 1. "anecdote"

Answer It refers to short entertaining story about a real person.

Question 2. "delicate realism"

Answer It refers to quality of the art which makes it seem real.

Question 3. "figurative painting"

Answer It refers to representation of a piece of art, through the eyes of the creator's imagination.

Question 4. "illusionistic likeness"

Answer It refers to technique of using pictorial methods to deceive the eye.

Question 5. "conceptual space"

Answer It refers to relation with the abstract instead of the factual representation, required for the understanding of concepts.

Understanding the text

Question 1.

(i) Contrast the Chinese view of art with the European with examples.

Answer The Chinese view of art is trying to achieve the essence of inner life and spirit. *E.g.,* Wu Dazoi's painting, which was commissioned by the emperor Xuanzong. While the emperor could only appreciate its outer brilliance, the artist entered his painting and disappeared alongwith his painting. This showed that emperor might have ruled his dynasty but the artist knew the ways within.

The European view of art is to create illusionistic likeness. *E.g.,* in 15th century a blacksmith had fallen in love with a painter's daughter. The father would not give his consent. The blacksmith entered the painter's studio and painted a fly on his latest panel with such realism that the painter almost swat it away before he realised what had happened. The painter then got his daughter married to him.

(ii) **Explain the concept of Shanshui.**

Answer   Shanshui literally means 'mountain water', which when used together represents the word 'landscape'. It reflects Daoist view of the universe which constitutes more than two elements of an image - Yang, the mountain, Yin - the water and the third element - middle void where the interaction of the mountain and water takes place.

Question 2.

(i) **What do you understand by the term 'outsider art' and 'art brut' on 'raw art'?**

Answer   The 'outsider art' is the art of those people who have no right to be the artists as they have received no formal training, yet they show talent and artistic insight.

The notion of 'art brut' or 'raw art' was of works that were in their raw state as regards cultural and artistic influence. Anything and everything from a tin to a sink to a broken car could be material for a work of art.

(ii) **Who was the untutored genius who created a paradise and what is the nature of his contribution to art?**

Answer   Nek Chand is the untutored genius who created a paradise years ago. The little patch of a jungle that he began clearing to make himself a garden, sculpted with stone and recycled material is known to the world as the 'Rock Garden' at Chandigarh. Nek Chand has taken the notion of raw art to dizzying heights. His art is, "an outstanding testimony of the difference a single man can make when he lives his dream".

Talking about the text

Discuss the following

Question 1. The emperor may rule over the territory he has conquered, but only the artist knows the way within.

Answer   The wonderful tale about the Chinese painter Wu Daozi proves the above statement substantially. His beautiful painting was commissioned by the emperor Xuanzong. When the painting was completed, the artist called the emperor to see. While the emperor was awed by its outer brilliance, the artist entered the painting and disappeared alongwith it, never to return. The tale denotes only the figurative meaning. For anyone to order for a beautiful creation is not a big deal but it is only the creator who understands its true beauty.

There is another way of interpreting this statement. While the emperors rule their territory, the artist transcends the boundaries and by the sheer beauty of his creations makes himself understand the universe. A great artist shows the way to go beyond any material appearance.

Question 2. The landscape is an inner one, a spiritual and conceptual place.

Answer The beauty of a creation can be understood in the truest sense by the mind and the heart, and not by the eyes alone. Only if one understands or reads the artist's mind, one can appreciate his work. A true artist does not want people to look at his art only from his angle. He gives them the freedom to interpret his work according to their own understanding.

The landscape is an inner one, a spiritual and conceptual place according to Shanshui, which is based on Daoist view. It is an interaction between Yang mountain and Yin water, and this interaction takes place in the middle void. This middle void is generally shown by the white or unpainted space. The role of the man also comes into play. He is the receiver of this communication and imagines or interprets this by his own understanding and becomes the 'eye of the landscape'.

Working with words

Question 1. The following common words are used in more than one sense.

| panel | studio | brush | essence | material |

Examine the following sets of sentences to find out what the words, 'panel' and 'essence' mean in different contexts.

A. (i) The masks from Bawa village in Mali look like long **panels** of decorated wood.

(ii) Judge H Hobart Grooms told the jury **panel** he had heard the reports.

(iii) The **panel** is laying the groundwork for an international treaty.

(iv) The glass **panels** of the window were broken.

(v) Through the many round tables, workshops and **panel** discussions, a consensus was reached.

(vi) The sink in the hinged **panel** above the bunk drains into the head.

Answer The meanings are (i) flat boards, (ii) group of men selected to give unanimous verdict on a legal case, (iii) small group of people made to decide some matter, (iv) sections, (v) group and (vi) section.

  B. (i) Their repetitive structure must have taught the people around the great composer the **essence** of music.

   (ii) Part of the answer is in the proposition; but the **essence** is in the meaning.

   (iii) The implications of these schools of thought are of practical **essence** for the teacher.

   (iv) They had added vanilla **essence** to the pudding.

Answer The meanings are (i) basic character and qualities, (ii) essential part, (iii) importance and (iv) extract from a plant or other substance used for flavouring.

Question 2. Now find five sentences each for the rest of the words to show the different senses in which each of them is used.

Answer
  1. Studio
   (i) The artist is working in his **studio** at home.
   (ii) The photographer's **studio** was full of his own photographs only.
   (iii) Kavita is learning classical dancing at the dance **studio** in Dwarka.
   (iv) All the actors in the scene must report in the film **studio** for shooting at 9 AM tomorrow.
   (v) James lives in a **studio** apartment in Mumbai.
  2. Brush
   (i) We should **brush** our teeth twice a day.
   (ii) Malvika is **brushing** a pink shade on her painting to complete it.
   (iii) A **brush** with death on the road is common for pedestrians in Delhi.
   (iv) Squirrel's **brushes** are used by expert painters for painting specific areas of a painting.
   (v) In an electric motor, graphite **brushes** are used to connect its coil with the electric supply.
  3. Material
   (i) Most persons today want only **material** pleasure.

(ii) Raw **material** for constructing earthquake proof buildings is very expensive.

(iii) Our winter trip to experience the snow in Shimla never **materialised**.

(iv) The selection committee members felt that Sunil was Test Match **material**; so they selected him.

(v) Comedy was an important **material** used by Shakespeare in many of his plays.

Noticing form

- A classical Chinese landscape is not meant to reproduce an actual view, as would a Western figurative painting.
- Whereas the European painter wants you to borrow his eyes and look at a particular landscape exactly as he saw it, from a specific angle, the Chinese painter does not choose a single viewpoint.

The above two examples are ways in which contrast may be expressed. Combine the following sets of ideas to show the contrast between them.

Question 1.   1

(i) European art tries to achieve a perfect, illusionistic likeness.

(ii) Asian art tries to capture the essence of inner life and spirit.

Answer While European art tries to achieve a perfect illusionistic likeness, Asian art tries to capture the essence of inner life and spirit.

Question 2.

(i) The Emperor commissions a painting and appreciates its outer appearance.

(ii) The artist reveals to him the true meaning of his work.

Answer Even though the Emperor commissions a painting and appreciates its outer appearance, it is the artist who reveals to him the true meaning of his work.

Question 3.

(i) The Emperor may rule over the territory he has conquered.

(ii) The artist knows the way within.

Answer Even though the Emperor rules over the territory he has conquered, it is the artist who knows the way within.

5

The Ailing Planet :
The Green
Movement's Role

Nani Palkhivala

Chapter Sketch

This lesson by 'Nani Palkivala' appeared in 'The Indian Express' in an article form, which was published on 24th November, 1994. In this lesson, he has raised the problems that the mother Earth faces. Steps have been taken to heal the ailing Earth in the form of the Green Movement but there is still a long way to go.

Green Movement The 'Green Movement' started in 1972 in New Zealand and since then it has gathered momentum.

The Story Retold

Acknowledgement that Earth is a living organism

Ccopernicus taught us that Earth and the other planets revolve round the Earth. Similarly, the Green Movement has brought this idea that Earth is a living organism, of which we are a part. Its needs should be preserved and protected.

The concept of sustainable development

The concept of sustainable development was popularised in 1987 by the World Commission on Environment and Development. It clearly states the idea that we should make developments for our present needs but we should be careful about the needs of the future generations as well.

The world's most dangerous animal

In a zoo at Lusaka (Zambia), there is cage, where we will not find any animal but a mirror to see our reflection and this cage carries a notice which reads, 'The world's most dangerous animal'. With the continuous and sustained efforts of a number of agencies in different countries, we, the human beings are realising that we should not dominate our mother Earth but respect her as a partner.

Brandt Commission

This was the first commission, which dealt with the question of ecology and environment. Mr LK Jha was a member of this commission. This commission raised the question whether we were to leave our successor planet of advancing deserts, impoverished landscapes and ailing environment.

Earth's principal biological systems

Mr Lester R Brown, in his book, 'The Global Economic Prospect' says that there are four principal biological systems-fisheries, forests grasslands and croplands. They not only supply our food requirements but also provide raw materials for the industry. The worrying factor is that mankind is staking unreasonable claim on these systems, which is bound to affect their productivity.

Article 48A of the Constitution of India

Note that it is the duty of the states to take efforts to improve the environment and safeguard the forests and wild life of the country. But, unfortunately, in this country, all the laws and rules are made to be broken. The glaring example of this law breaking tendency is untouchability, casteism and bonded labour that are prevalent even today. The alarming rate at which the forests are depleting is another example of how laws are treated in India.

The menace of over population

The growth of world population is one of the strongest factors in shadowing the future. Every four days, the world population increases by one million. The population of India is more than the entire populations of Africa and South America together. More children do not mean more workers, it merely means more people without work. The only solution to this is voluntary family planning.

Era of Responsibility

Slowly but steadily, people are understanding the concept that the entire world should be treated as an integrated whole rather than the separated collection of parts. For a sustainable development of the world, every one has to play its role, even the industries. Margaret Thatcher and Lester Brown suggested that this Earth is not our property. It passes on from one generation to another with the hope that each generation will take care of it so as to pass on to the next, with resources intact.

Exercises

Notice these expressions

Notice these expressions in the text. Infer their meaning from the context.

Question 1. a holistic and ecological view

Answer   a complete and comprehensive view of ecology which takes into account all species

Question 2. sustainable development

Answer   development that takes care of the present needs and ensures at the same time that there are enough resources for the future generation

Question 3. languish

Answer   remain unnoticed

Question 4. ignominious darkness

Answer   to remain in the dark in a humiliating manner

Question 5. inter alia

Answer   among other things

Question 6. decimated

Answer   reduced drastically

Question 7. catastropic depletion

Answer   disastrous reduction in number

Question 8. transcending concern

Answer main anxiety or worry

Understanding the text

Question 1. Locate the lines in the text that support the title, 'The Ailing Planet'.

Answer "The Earth's vital signs reveal a patient in declining health" are the lines that support the title 'The Ailing Planet'.

Question 2. What does the notice, 'the world's most dangerous animal' at a cage in the zoo at Lusaka, Zambia, signify?

Answer In a zoo at Lusaka, Zambia, there is a cage where the notice reads, 'the world's most dangerous animal'. Inside the cage, there is no animal but a mirror where one sees one's own reflection. This notice signifies that our planet faces the most potential threat from mankind rather from any other animal. Basically, it is man who thinks that Earth is his property and he can dominate it in any way he likes, eroding its resources to fulfill his selfish needs.

Question 3. How are the earth's principal biological systems being depleted?

Answer There are four principal biological systems of the Earth - (1) fisheries (2) forests (3) grasslands (4) croplands, as pointed by Mr Lester R Brown. Unfortunately, the human claims on these systems as reaching points, where their productivity is getting impaired. The protein hungry world is over-fishing everyday.

In poor countries, local forests are being destroyed everyday to get firewood for cooking. The growing use of dung for burning deprives the soil of an important natural fertilizer. The forests precede mankind and deserts follow. The world's tropical forests are eroding at the rate of forty to fifty millions acres per year. Also, grasslands and croplands are being converted into deserts and wastelands.

Question 4. Why does the author over that the growth of world population is one of the strongest factors distorting the future of human society?

Answer According to the author, it took mankind more than a million years to reach the first billion. This was around the year 1800. But in the 21st century, the world's population reached to an estimate of 5.7 billion. Every four days, the world population increases by one million. More children does not mean more hands to work, merely more people without work. No sustainable development can take place till population explosion is put under control. The choice is between control of population and perpetuation of poverty.

Talking about the text

Question 1. Laws are never respected nor enforced in India.discuss

Answer It is, indeed, a very sad state of affairs that in India, laws are neither respected nor enforced. There is a very well-written Constitution of India that covers all the aspects of the running of a country. Everyday, the laws are made and reforms take place. But generally, Indians believe in breaking the laws or interpreting them according to their convenience. Take an *e.g.,* dowry, child labour or female infanticide.

There is a general apathy towards the system, which is required to enforce the law. There could be a lot of reasons behind this. Corruption is on the top. We, in India, know that everyone and everything is on sale. Second reason could be that, in our country, the course of justice takes a lot of time. We believe in the fact that, 'Justice delayed is justice denied'. So, there is a possibility that, here, people take law in their hands and try to meet their demands according to the way they want to.

Question 2. Are we to leave our successors a scorched planet of advancing deserts, impoverished landscapes and an ailing environment? Discuss.

Answer The ever-rising inflation, the high cost of living, paucity of drinking water, frequent power cuts 'these are the problems we face everyday. We fall sick with so many new ailments. These are the assets we have inherited from our ancestors. But the question is, if we are suffering, should we not think of finding solutions to these problems and give a better world to our successors?

We, certainly, have to take corrective measures to ensure that we do not leave our successors a scorched planet of advancing deserts, impoverished landscape and an ailing environment. We should not make unreasonable claims on the four biological systems (1) fisheries (2) forests (3) grasslands (4) croplands. Overfishing should be avoided and forests should be preserved. New plants should be planted. We should try to avoid using cow dung for burning, so as not to deprive soil of its natural fertilizer.

Question 3. We have not inherited this Earth from our fore-fathers. We have borrowed it from our children. Discuss

Answer The Mother Earth is not our ancestral property. We cannot make undue claims on her. In our foolhardiness, we try to deplete the natural resources without realising how it is going to affect our progeny. The fruits that we eat today are the products of a tree, which was not planted by us. We have to base our thought process on the similar line. What we sow today, our next generation will reap tomorrow.

Our Earth is not our legacy. In the words of Margaret Thatcher, "No generation has a freehold on this Earth". All we have is a life tenancy with a full repairing lease. We should take care of Earth's resources as a borrowed thing. We neither can over use it nor can we neglect it. We have to return it to the next generation without any damage and, if possible, with further addition of its life-giving resources.

Question 4. The problems of over population that directly affect our everyday life. Discuss.

Answer There is no doubt that the growth of world population is one of the strongest factors distorting the future of human society.

World population is increasing at a rapid speed. Every four days, the world population increases by one million. This is a very alarming situation. Everyday, we face the brunt of this menace. There is not a single utility place, where there are not big queues be it a hospital, ration shops or educational institutes.

Over population makes poor still poorer. More children do not mean more hands to work. It only means less work and more mouths to feed. All around us, faces this problem. There are not enough houses for everyone, so we find slums everywhere. In government hospitals, where the treatment is available at a reduced cost, there are not enough beds for the patients. Everyday, there are new colleges, schools opening up, but still the rate of illiteracy is not dropping down. Unless strict measures are taken to control population, we are heading for a big trouble.

Thinking about language

The phrase 'inter alia' meaning 'among other things' is one of many Latin expressions commonly used in English.

Find out what these Latin phrases mean.

1. *prima facie*   2. *ad hoc*

3. *in camera*   4. *ad infinitum*

5. *mutatis mutandis*   6. *caveat*

7. *tabula rasa*

Answer

1. **prima facie** at first sight, before closer inspection
2. **ad hoc** for the specific purpose, case, or situation at hand and for no other, temporary
3. **in camera** in secret, in private
4. **ad infinitum** to infinity, having no end
5. **mutatis mutandis** having substituted new terms, the necessary changes having been made
6. **caveat** warning or caution
7. **tabula rasa** blank slate, an opportunity for a fresh start

Working with words

Question 1. Locate the following phrases in the text and study their connotation.

1. gripped the imagination of
2. dawned upon
3. ushered in
4. passed into the current coin
5. passport for the future

Answer

1. **gripped the imagination of** received much attention
2. **dawned upon** realised for the first time
3. **ushered in** introduced something, began a new idea
4. **passed into the current coin** been brought into use
5. **passport for the future** permit for taking us to a brighter future

Question 2. The words 'grip', 'dawn', 'usher', 'coin', 'passport' have a literal as well as a figurative meaning. Write pairs of sentences using each word in the literal as well as the figurative sense.

Answer

1. **grip**

    Literal The baby *gripped* my finger with her tiny hand.

    Figurative The movement of 'India Against Corruption' had *gripped* the minds of Indians.

2. **dawn**
   Literal We walked all night and reached the station at *dawn*.
   Figurative Suddenly, the idea *dawned* on him.
3. **usher**
   Literal The waiter *ushered* them to their seats.
   Figurative The Green Movement *ushered* in a new era of awareness.
4. **coin**
   Literal I have five *coins* of ₹10.
   Figurative The term was *coined* by a famous philosopher.
5. **passport**
   Literal Finally she got her *passport* made to visit her daughter in Germany.
   Figurative Education is the *passport* to a bright future.

6

The Browning Version

Terence Rattigan

Chapter Sketch

This lesson by 'Terrence Rattigan is an act play set in a school. Taplow, a sixteen year old boy, is waiting for his master Crocker-Harris, who has asked him to do some extra work. As Taplow is waiting for his master, another teacher, Frank, arrives. Frank and Taplow get into a conversation.

The Story Retold

Taplow waits for his master Crocker-Harris when Frank arrives

Taplow has been asked to do some extra work by Crocker-Harris. While he is waiting for him, another master, Frank, arrives. He asks Taplow if he knows him. Taplow replies in negative. On his further enquiry, Taplow tells him that he is in lower fifth standard and is waiting for his results. Frank is surprised that Taplow does not know his results. He says that he is well aware of the **rule** that form results are only be announced by the headmaster on the last day of the term. Taplow says, it is only Mr Crocker-Harris who abides by this rule and, perhaps, no one else.

Taplow's inclination towards Sscience

Frank enquiries whether Taplow would prefer to take science as a subject after clearing. Taplow, with all enthusiasm replies that he, definitely, would like to go for Science as he is not interested in literature, where he would be asked to read plays like Agamemnon. Frank is surprised to hear Taplow calling Agamemnon a muck. Taplow explains that there is nothing wrong with the play but he is not happy with the way it is been taught.

Taplow's bad mood and his criticism of his master Crocker-Harris

Frank asks Taplow the reason for his a little bitter feeling. Taplow says that he does not like to do extra work at a time when he play golf. He further explains that, Crocker-Harris is leaving the day after for good, but he has insisted that Taplow should do the work because he had missed a day last week due to illness. Frank tries to comfort him by saying that taking extra work might help in improving his grades. Taplow comes out openly in his criticism and says that Crocker-Harris is not the type who would give extra marks on extra work.

Taplow's veiled appreciation of his master Crocker-Harris

Taplow tells Frank that he asked Mr Crocker Harris if he would be getting extra marks for doing extra work. The master replied that he would be getting only what he deserves, no less no more. He recounts this to Frank imitating Crocker-Harris and he further adds that Mr Crocker-Harris is hardly a human. When Frank chides him he feels apologetic. When Frank advises him to go and play golf since Crocker-Harris is late, Taplow refuses saying that if he goes, the master would follow him home.

Frank feels envious of Crocker-Harris for having such an effect on his students. He asks Taplow if Crocker-Harris beat his students. Taplow immediately denies it and says that Crocker-Harris is not a sadist like one or two other masters. He asks Frank if he knows the meaning of sadist since he was a science teacher. The way Taplow put across his views, shocks Frank.

The unusual personality of Crocker-Harris

According to Taplow, Mr Crocker Harris cannot be a sadist. For being a sadist, one has to have some feelings but Crocker-Harris is devoid of any feelings. He seems to hate people who like him. Taplow confesses to Frank that inspite of all these weird qualities, he rather likes his master, and funnily enough, he (Crocker Harris) sees it and shrivels even further.

Taplow mocks his master in front of Frank

Taplow tells Frank that a few days ago, Crocker Harris made one of his classical jokes in the class. No one laughed because none could understand and, out of sheer courtesy, Taplow laughed. Crocker-Harris complimented him by saying that his understanding of Latin has improved that helped him to understand the joke. Crocker-Harris thin insisted that he should explain the joke to the rest of the class so that all of them would share the pleasure.

Crocker-Harris' wife enters

Millie, Crocker-Harris' wife, is a thin woman and smartly dressed up. She closes the door and watches Taplow and Frank, who are engrossed in the conversation. They noticed her only after a little time has passed.

The ensuing conversation between Millie and Taplow

It is Frank who noticed Millie first. Taplow is a little worried about Millie overhearing their conversation. He asks Frank about the possibility and Frank confirms his fears saying that she was standing there for quiet some time. After the exchange of pleasantaries, Millie asks Taplow if he was waiting for her husband.

When Taplow confirms, she informs him that he is at the Brusar's and might be there for quite sometime. She asks him to leave. Taplow refuses because the master had particularly asked him to stay. She, then, asks him to go for half an hour. Taplow is again doubtful. She takes a prescription out of the basket and asks him to go to the chemist and get it made up. Taplow consents and departs.

Exercises

Notice these expressions

Notice these expressions in the text. Infer their meaning from the context.

Question 1. remove

Answer promotion to the next class

Question 2. slackers

Answer lazy, careless, unmotivated students

Question 3. muck

Answer rubbish, useless

Question 4. kept in

Answer detained, held back to stay after school hours

Question 5. got carried away

Answer got very excited

Question 6. cut

Answer go away without permission

Question 7. sadist

Answer a person who gets pleasure out of inflicting pain to others

Question 8. shrivelled up

Answer having no feelings

Understanding the text

Question 1. Comment on the attitude shown by Taplow towards Crocker Harris.

Answer From his conversation with Frank, it appears that Taplow does not think too high of his master, Crocker-Harris. He says that Crocker-Harris is, probably, the only teacher who adheres to the rules, which apparently do not suit Taplow. Mr Crocker-Harris does not have any sense of humour and he hates when people like him. However, in between the dialogues, he also says something very positive about his teacher. Taplow says that Crocker-Harris is not the kind of teacher who will give any extra marks for any extra work and he is not a sadist. He even confesses that he rather likes his master. This shows that he also harbours some respect for his strict master.

Question 2. Does Frank seem to encourage Taplow's comments on Crocker-Harris?

Answer Yes, Frank seems to encourage Taplow's comments on Crocker-Harris. First of all, he does not make any sincere effort to stop Taplow from passing disparaging comments about Crocker-Harris. Secondly, he eggs him on when Taplow is talking about the negative qualities of his master.

Question 3. What do you gather about Crocker-Harris from the play?

Answer Crocker-Harris is a school master, who is about to leave the school for good. According to the play, he seems to be an unbiased, strict and honest teacher. He is a believer of the principle that every student should get what he/she deserves - neither more, nor less. He does not like it when people admire him. The fact is that, his qualities as a teacher, are superb, hence, even a student like Taplow has hidden admiration for him.

Talking about the text

Discuss

Question 1. Talking about teachers among friends.

Answer The most common trait among students is to talk about their teachers. Students have tremendous capacity to analyse the qualities (good or bad) of their teachers. Even a dumb student can understand, whether if a teacher is proficient in his subject or not. That is the reason, after each class, students form groups and discuss what had happened in the foregone period.

Students, generally, pass comments on the teachers' appearance also. A well-dressed and smartly turned out teacher is always appreciated by the students. If one listens to the comments of the students one could easily decipher one fact-a teacher who is however strict but honest and unbiased, and knows his subject will definitely earn from his students. Nothing is more important for students, than a teacher's ability to make them understand their subject.

Question 2. The manner you adopt, when you talk about a teacher to other teachers.

Answer We are always very guarded in voicing our opinions about a teacher when we talk to other teachers. First of all, we are never very sure that our comments about a teacher will not be passed to him/her by others. We always have this lingering doubt that, afterall, these teachers work together and their work culture demands to be interactive with their colleagues.

Sometimes, we come across some teachers who ask mis-leading questions about other teachers as we saw in the lesson 'The Browning Version'. Frankly, it appears as if Frank was restricting Taplow to pass uncharitable comments on Crocker-Harris but, in fact, he wanted him to give a comprehensive report of Crocker-Harris.

In similar circumstances, sometimes we lose our guard and say things about other teachers that may or may not be appropriate. One thing that all of us should understand is that before passing negative comments on our teachers', we have to ensure whom we are talking to.

Question 3. Reading plays is more interesting than studying science.

Answer It is very true because fiction, always, is more interesting than facts. Plays may be based on true stories but the writer, with the help of his imagination, gives it a creative description. On the other hand, science deals only with facts. There is no scope for creativity. One can add or subtract to come to a solution but the basics can never be changed.

Sometimes, it is true but it depends on one's view point. There are a lot of people who would like to deal with facts only. For them, plays are just a timepass. One reads them in leisure hours to relax. Reading plays would not provide solutions to any problem. Science, which is based on true findings, only can be the answer to the problems, which we face in our daily life. This view point is very subjective. Some of us like reading plays while others like science.

Working with words

A sadist is a person who gets pleasure out of giving pain to others.

Given below are some dictionary definitions of certain kinds of persons. Find out the words that fit these descriptions.

Question 1. A person who considers it very important that things should be correct or genuine e.g. in the use of language or in the arts.

Answer Perfectionist

Question 2. A person who believes that war and violence are wrong and will not fight in a war.

Answer   Pacifist

Question 3. A person who believes that nothing really exists.

Answer   Nihilist

Question 4. A person who is always hopeful and expects the best in all things.

Answer   Optimist

Question 5. A person who follows generally accepted norms of behaviour.

Answer   Conformist

Question 6. A person who believes that material possessions are all that matter in life.

Answer   Materialist

7

The Adventure

Jayant Narlikar

Chapter Sketch

The story deals with the strange way our mind works. Sometimes, a small event triggers our mind in such a way that it appears that we are either travelling down a memory lane or have jumped across the future. In reality, neither we venture into the past nor into the future, but remain in the present, experiencing a different world.

The Story Retold

The journey of Professor Gaitonde to Bombay by Jijamata Express

Professor Gaitonde was travelling to Bombay from Pune by Jijamata Express, which was faster than Deccan Queen. Professor was trying to form a plan of action, once he reached Bombay. He was contemplating how the present affairs reached such a state. He intended to return to Pune and have a long discussion with Rajendra Deshpande. The train stopped at Sarhad where an Anglo-Indian railway officer checked the permits of the passengers.

The conversation between Gangadhar Pant and Khan Sahib

Khan Sahib was a co-passenger, who was going Peshawar *via* Delhi and Lahore. They entered into a conversation. Khan Sahib spoke at length about his business. Gangadhar Pant listened attentively because he wanted to know about the life, which was so different from his.

Slowly, the train passed through the suburban rail traffic, where on the carriages it was written GBMR (Great Bombay Metropolitan Railway) Khan Sahib explained that they were in the British territory.

Gangadhar Pant gets a shock

When the train stopped at Victoria Terminus, Gangadhar Pant got out of the station and found a huge building. The building was headquarters of the East India Company. He thought that after the Revolt of 1857 the East India Company wound up. But that was incorrect. Here, it was alive and prospering. He thought, perhaps, history had taken a different turn. As he walked along Hornby Road, he found all the British departmental stores and offices of British banks.

Professor Gaitonde's failure to meet his son

Professor Gaitonde entered Forbes building and asked the English receptionist if he could meet Vinay Gaitonde. The receptionist informed him that no such employee worked in any of the branches of Forbes. He was shocked. His mind was more focused on going to Town Hall where the library of the Asiatic Society could help him to solve the problems of history, which, according to him, had taken a different turn.

Professor read five volumes of history on the Town Hall library

Gangadhar Pant went to Town Hall library and asked for a list of historic books including his own. He read all the five volumes. In volume V, he finally found the point where the history had taken a different turn.

The page described the Battle of Panipat, where Marathas had won and Abdali was chased back to Kabul. The book did not give a detailed account of the battle. It was rather about the consequences of the battle and the power struggle. This was Gangadhar Pant's own version. He was the author.

The victory of Panipat as viewed by Gangadhar Pant

Because of the victory of Marathas in Panipat, the East India Company had to forego its expansion programme. Vishwasrao was a powerful Maratha ruler. He and his brother, Madhavrao, were shrewd politicians and increased their influence all over India. The East India Company was confined to Bombay, Calcutta and Madras.

For political reasons, the Peshwas kept the Mughal rule in Delhi. The technological age was dawning in Europe. East India Company saw this as another opportunity to exercise its influence. but their expertise was restricted only to the local centres.

The twentieth century saw a lot of changes under the Western influence. India moved towards democracy. Peshwas lost their influence and were replaced by democratic elected bodies. The Mughal ruler in Delhi survived all these upheavals because, in reality, he was only a rubber stamp.

Gangadhar Pant's appreciation of India that he has seen

As Gangadhar Pant read futrther, he started appreciating India which had learnt to be self-reliant and not be dominated by white men. From a strong position, it had reduced the British to retain Bombay as the sole outpost, according to a treaty which was to expire in 2001.

Gangadhar Pant feels his investigations are incomplete

The professor compared the country he knew with what he was witnessing around. He felt that he did not know the complete history. He wanted to find how Marathas won the battle. He knew that answers could be found in the account of the battle itself. He went through all the books and journals till he found the one by Bhausahebanchi Bakhar, which gave him the clue he was looking for.

He seldom relied on the doctored account of the book but in the book he found about how Vishwasrao got killed. The librarian, at 8 pm, requested the professor that it was time to close the library. As the professor was getting out of the library, he mistakenly shoved Bakhar into his pocket.

Gangadhar Pant's visit to Azad Maidan

Gangadhar Pant found a guest house to stay and after eating, he walked towards Azad Maidan. There, he found a meeting was about to take place. He was surprised that the presidential chair was vacant for the meeting. He moved towards it. The speaker on the dias stopped speaking and the audience started shouting. The professor tried his best to convince the audience that there should be a president presiding over the audience and this should not be an unchaired lecture but the audience would not listen.

They remarked that they were tired of sick remarks, introduction, vote of thanks etc. from the usual presidential chair and they wanted to hear only the speakers. Professor was in no mood to listen. The audience then targeted him with eggs and tomatoes and, finally, threw him off the stage. In the crowd, Gangadhar Pant disappeared.

Professor narrates his experience to Rajendra Deshpande

When professor talked about his two days experience to Rajendra, he was speechless. He asked professor what he was doing when he met with an accident with the truck two days ago. Professor replied that he was thinking of catastrophe theory and its consequences on history.

Gangadhar Pant produced a torn page from the Bakhar as an evidence that he was not imagining things as Rajendra thought. When Rajendra read that, he told the professor that until then he had thought that professor was fantasising the experience but he was convinced that certain facts were stranger than fantasy.

Rajendra's explanation of catastrophic theory

Rajendra tried to explain the catastropic experience that professor Gaitonde had undgergone. He tried to rationalise it by relating it to the Battle of Panipat. In the Battle of Panipat, Maratha army and Abdalis' troops were at par in all the aspects. All depended on the leadership. The killing of Vishwasrao, the son and heir of Peshwa, proved to be the turning point. His uncle Bhausaheb rushed, never to be seen again.

The Marathas lost their spirit of fighting. Then, Rajendra tried to explain what professor had read on the torn page from Bakhar when the bullet missed Vishwasrao. Things would have been different if this was true that Vishwasrao survived. The idea "it might have been" is food for contemplation but not for reality. He further explained that reality may not be unique.

Scientists had established this through the experiments on very small systems of atoms and their constituent particles. The experiment came out with an astonishing finding. The behaviour of these systems could not be predicted as definite even if all the laws governing these systems were known.

With a Bullet, one can be sure that it will reach its target, but with an electron, no such assertion can be made. Professor Gaitonde understood this lack of determinism in quantum theory.

Gangadhar Pant's dawning realisation

Gangadhar Pant tried to understand this further when Rajendra explained again. The world may have many pictures. In one world, electron is found in one place and in another, it is found in a different place. According to where the electron lands, there can be co-existence of many different worlds.

It is not simple as the theory of planets revolving round the Sun. The movement of electrons is not precise. They can jump from a higher state of energy to a lower state of energy and *vice-versa*. Gangadhar Pant understood this. He made a transition from one world to another and back again. He was able to experience two worlds, one that has the known history, another what could have been.

He understood about the transition but the question that bothered him was, why he did that. Rajendra, though, did not have a definite answer to this, he speculated that some kind of interaction had made this transition. When the professor met with an accident, he was wondering about the Battle of Panipat. He then informed Rajendra about his decision not to preside at any other meeting. He had conveyed his regrets to the organiser of the Panipat Seminar.

Exercises

Notice these expressions

Question 1. "blow-by-blow account"

Answer It refers to detailed description.

Question 2. "morale booster"

Answer It refers to event that improved their confidence and raised their morale.

Question 3. "relegated to"

Answer It refers to assigned to a lower rank or position.

Question 4. "political acumen"

Answer It refers to political shrewdness with keen insight.

Question 5. *"de facto"*

Answer It refers to existing.

Question 6. "astute"

Answer It refers to marked by practical intelligence.

Question 7. "doctored accounts"

Answer It refers to narratives changed so as to deceive.

Question 8. "gave vent to"

Answer It refers to expressed his feelings and ideas.

Understanding the text

Question 1. Tick the statements that are true.
1. The story is an account of real events.
2. The story hinges on a particular historical event.
3. Rajendra Deshpande was a historian.
4. The places mentioned in the story are all imaginary.
5. The story tries to relate history to science.

Answer   1. False   2. True   3. False   4. False
            5. True

Question 2. Briefly explain the following statements from the text.

1. "You neither travelled to the past nor the future. You were in the present experiencing a different world."

   Answer These lines were spoken by Rajendra Deshpande when he was trying to give an explanation for Professor Gaitonde's strange experience. When professor met with an accident, he was thinking about the Battle of Panipat and its consequences. His mind travelled between the history we know and what could have been. By making a transition, professor was able to experience two worlds, although one at a time. By the same theory, there must be many more different worlds arising out of bifurcations at different points of time.

2. You have passed through a fantastic experience : or more correctly, a catastrophic experience."

   Answer Rajendra Deshpande told Professor Gaitonde that he passed through a very fantastic experience. He explained that we lived in a unique world, which had a unique history. The idea 'it might have been' was fine for speculation but not for reality. Due to the accident, Gangadhar Pant's mind jumped on to another world, which could have been. In that world, history took a different turn as

Marathas won the Battle of Panipat. Rajenera explained this through catastrophic theory, according to which reality has many manifestations.

3. **"Gangadhar Pant could not help comparing the country he knew with what he was witnessing around him."**

   Answer In his extraordinary experience, Gangadhar Pant witnessed two different manifestations of the same reality, although one at a time. The India he knew was described in the history books on the basis of the Battle of Panipat of 1761 , where Marathas were defeated. The other India that he saw was the result of the victory of Marathas in the battle. In this version, he saw India as a self-reliant ant and prosperous country.

4. **The lack of determinism in quantum theory.**

   Answer If a bullet is fired from a gun in a given direction at a given speed, one will know where it will be later, but such an assertion cannot be made for an electron. When an electron is fired from a source, it may be here, there, anywhere. This is lack of determinism in quantum theory. This theory asserts that reality is never one-sided. Alternative worlds may exist at the same time.

5. **You need some interaction to cause a transition.**

   Answer Professor Gaintonde made a transition, which according to Rajendra Deshpande, had happened because of the interaction happening in the professor's mind at the time of collision. When the collision took place, professor was thinking about catastrophe theory and its role in wars. May be, he was wondering about the Battle of Panipat and its consequences. The interaction in his brain acted as a trigger to cause a transition.

Talking about the text

Question 1.

(i) **A single event may change the course of the history of a nation. Discuss.**

   Answer **In Favour** The history of a nation takes long to develop but this history may, suddenly, take a new course by a single event happening in a particular moment. This can be reinstated by the Battle of Panipat. When the Maratha Army faced the troops of Abdali, there was no disparity between the two. Only the leadership could have made the difference. At a crucial juncture, Vishwasrao, the son and heir of Peshwa was killed. His uncle Bhausaheb also could not survive. For Marathas, losing their leader was a blow and Abdali won.

In fact, the Battle of Panipat was the beginning of the subjugation of our country.

Against It is very difficult to believe that a single event can change any nation's history. True, Marathas lost the Battle of Panipat and it had severe consequences on India, then. But there were subsequent factors, which made us slaves for a very long duration. The Britishers wilfully followed the 'Divide and Rule' policy and ruled us for years together. A single event can affect an individual's life but to change the history of a nation, one requires a significant chain of events to happen.

(ii) **Reality is what is directly experienced through sense. Discuss**

Answer **In Favour** Reality, indeed, is what is directly experienced through senses. It is limited to what we see. The proverb "seeing is believing" has taken its true flavour from this reality only. We appreciate beauty with our eyes. We hear with our ears. Because of the direct experience of our senses, we are able to decipher between good and bad objects. Gangadhar Pant had to undergo that strange experience because his mind was in the denial mode of what his senses were perceiving.

Against The mind works on different levels. It is not necessary that what we see may not be the true in reality. That is why, we have coined the term 'Illusionistic Reality'. Sometimes, the reality is experienced through indirect instruments also. In the case of professor Gaitonde, he perceived reality indirectly. He saw reality in terms of 'What could have been' or 'should be'. What his senses perceived was the reality he was seeing. That proves that reality has other manifestations also.

(iii) **The methods of inquiry of History, Science and Philosophy are similar. Discuss.**

Answer **In Favour** The methods of inquiry of History, Science and Philosophy are similar in the sense that all the three deals with reality. If we have to know the facts, either historic, scientific or philosophical, we have to adopt the research method. All the three have written accounts, which are proved practically. Battle of Panipat was fought and lost by Marathas. History proves that the mind can perceive two-three worlds at the same time as proved by lack of determinism in quantum theory. It is a proven scientific theory. 'The mind perceives what it wants to perceive,' is a philosophical theory, which is reinstated in the lesson, 'The Adventure, through Gangadhar' Pant's experience.

Against The methods of inquiry for History, Science and Philosophy are not the same. What has already gone is History. Why did a few things happen and how new things can be made to happen is science. Philosophy deals with idealism, "What it should be". Battle of Panipat a much talked about incident is history. We read and re-read about it in History books. Gangadhar Pant's fantastic experience and his transition to another world is the journey of his mind, which can be attributed to the catastrophe theory of science. His mind's journey to an ideal world, where he sees India as he wants to see it is philosophy. The fundamental base of Philosophy, Science and History may be the same but the approach is radically different.

Question 2.

(i) The story is called "The Adventure" Compare it to the adventure described in "We Are Not Afraid to Die."

Answer   The underlying theme of both the stories, "The Adventure" and "We Are Not Afraid to Die" is the same. However, the execution is very different. One deals with the adventure in a real life situation and the other one is about the adventure that was mentally experienced. In the story, "We Are Not Afraid to Die", the characters take a hazardous sea voyage, to overcome the odds and survive. Whatever the dangers were, they were very real. In the story, 'The Adventure", the protagonist does not embark upon an adventurous journey. His collision with the truck triggers his mind to travel to a world, which is different from the world that he lives in.

(ii) Why do you think Professor Gaitonde decided never to preside over meetings again?

Answer   Professor Gaitonde realised that whatever he has experienced was based on what he was thinking at the time of his accident. Rajendra Deshpandes' explanation satisfied him. Through his other world experience, he also understood the fact that the president in a meeting is not welcomed by the audience. They are only interested in listening to the speakers. Hence, he decided never to preside over meetings again.

Thinking about language

Question 1.   In which language do you think Gangadharpant and Khan Sahib talked to each other? Which language did Gangadharpant use to talk to the English receptionist?

Answer   Gangadharpant and Khan Sahib would have talked in Hindi or Hindustani, as both of them are educated and speaking fluently to each other. Gangadharpant must have used English to talk to the English receptionist.

Question 2.   In which language do you think *Bhausahebanchi Bakhar* was written?

Answer *Bhausahebanchi Bakhar* was written in the Marathi language, as the words are Marathi words and *Bakhar* is a form of historical narrative written in Marathi prose.

Question 3. There is mention of three communities in the story: the Marathas, the Mughals, the Anglo-Indians. Which language do you think they used within their communities and while speaking to the other groups?

Answer Within their communities, the Marathas would have spoken in Marathi, the Mughals in Urdu and the Anglo-Indians in English. While speaking to the other groups, they would have used the services of interpreters who were fluent in both languages to translate what was said into the language of the listener.

Question 4. Do you think that the ruled always adopt the language of the ruler?

Answer No, they do not because a new language would be difficult to learn, especially if it is written in a different script. This is the case here, as Marathi, English and Urdu are written in three different scripts.

Working with words

Question 1. Tick the item that is closest in meaning to the following phrases.

(i) to take issue with

(a) to accept   (b) to discuss

(c) to disagree   (d) to add

Answer (c) to disagree

(ii) to give vent to

(a) to express   (b) to emphasise

(c) suppress   (d) dismiss

Answer (a) to express

(iii) to stand on one's feet

(a) to be physically strong   (b) to be independent

(c) to stand erect   (d) to be successful

Answer (b) to be independent

(iv) to be wound up

    (a) to become active   (b) to stop operating

    (c) to be transformed   (d) to be destroyed

Answer   (b) to stop operating

(v) to meet one's match

    (a) to meet a partner who has similar tastes

    (b) to meet an opponent

    (c) to meet someone who is equally able as oneself

    (d) to meet defeat

Answer   (c) to meet someone who is equally able as oneself

Question 2. Distinguish between the following pairs of sentences.

(i) (a) He was visibly moved.

    (b) He was visually impaired.

Answer Sentence (a) means that the concerned person's behaviour was perceptibly affected. Sentence (b) means that the concerned person's sight was perceptibly affected, i.e., he was partially or fully blind.

(ii) (a) Green and black stripes were used alternately.

    (b) Green stripes could be used or alternatively black ones.

Answer Sentence (a) means that green and black stripes were used one after the other. Sentence (b) means that either green stripes could be used or black ones.

(iii) (a) The team played the two matches successfully.

    (b) The team played two matches successively.

Answer Sentence (a) means that the team played two matches with success, i.e., they won both the matches. Sentence (b) means that the team played two matches one after another.

(iv) (a) The librarian spoke respectfully to the learned scholar.

    (b) You will find the historian and the scientist in the archaeology and natural science sections of the museum respectively.

Answer Sentence (a) means that the librarian spoke with respect to the learned scholar. Sentence (b) means that one will find the historian in the archaeology section and the scientist in the natural science section of the museum.

8

Silk Road

Nick Middleton

Chapter Sketch

The author 'Nick Middleton', in the lesson 'Silk Road' writes about his journey to Mount Kailash, the travails of this difficult journey, the sensitive behaviour of hill folk and the accounts of exotic places in legends and the reality.

The Story Retold

The author's start of the journey to Mansarovar

It was a perfect morning in Ravu, when the author decided to leave for Mansarovar to complete kora.

Lhamo gave him a long-sleeved sheepskin coat. The author, along with Daniel and Tsetan, took a short cut to get off Changtang.

On the route, they meet Kyang, Drokbas and Nomad's dark tents

From the rolling hills of Ravu, they came where the plains became more stony than grassy. Here, they saw a great herd of wild ass. Tsetan said, 'Kyang' and pointed towards a far-off pall of dust, which made them see these asses long before they actually appeared. After some time, they passed solitary drokbas tending their flocks. Sometimes, these drokbas paused and stared at their car. They passed through nomad's dark tents, pitched in total isolation guarded by huge, black dog-a Tibetan Mastiff.

Guard dogs-a Tibetan Mastiff

These guard dogs were like beasts. They would stare right in the eyes and as the author and his companions drew closer, they exploded into action, directly towards them like a bullet from a gun. These ferocious animals wore bright red collars and barked furiously. They did not fear the vehicle. Tsetan, the driver, had to brake and severe several times. The fierce dogs made sure that the author and his companions were successfully chased off from the property. The author understood why these mastiff were popular in China's imperial courts.

The author's entry in a valley

As the author speed on, he could see snow capped mountains. His companion and he entered a valley, where the river was mostly clogged with ice. They slowly gained height. There were steeper slopes. The author felt the pressure building up on his ears. Suddenly, Tsetan stopped and jumped out of his seat. Daniel followed suit.

The start of the difficulties

The snow lay across the track and continued on both the sides making the bank too steep for the vehicle to climb. All the three started slithering and sliding forward. They were at 5,210 metres above the sea level. Tsetan gathered handful of dirt and flung it on the frozen surface. When the soil was spread over snow, Tsetan drove towards the dirty snow and eased the car onto its surface. Daniel and the author walked to lighten the load of the car. After sometime, they stopped at another blockage. The slope was steep and was full of big rocks. Somehow, Tsetan managed and they drove on.

When they crept past 5,400 metres, the author's head began to throb and he had to take water. Finally, they reached the top of the pass at 5,515 metres. There, they saw large rocks, which were covered with white scarves and ragged prayer flags. After doing a traditional turn of these rocks, they started. By two o'clock, they stopped for lunch in a work camp beside a dry salt lake. This plateau was a hub of activity. Salt extraction from the lake was in full swing.

The travellers reached the small town of Hor

They reached the small town on the main East-West highway that followed the old trade route from Lhasa to Kashmir. Daniel hiked a ride in a truck to Lhasa. The author and Daniel bade him farewell. The two tyres that had got punctured, also, were replaced.

Hor was a grim and miserable place. There were only dust and rocks. The place was in a bad state, which was unfortunate since the town was on the shore of lake Mansarovar. According to ancient Hindu mythology, Mansarovor was the source of four great Indian rivers— the Ganges, the Sutlej, the Indus and the Brahamputra.

In fact, only the Sutlej flows from the lake. The author was very close to the mountain and wanted to continue his journey.

Author's disappointment with Hor

Though the author wanted to go ahead, he had to wait. He went to have a cup of coffee in the only cafe over there. The author's experience of Hor was a stark contrast to the account by earlier travellers. Ekai Kawaguchi, a Japanese monk, who had arrived there in 1900 was so moved by the sight of the lake that he burst into tears. Sven Hadin, a Swede, later on experienced similar effects.

The author reaches Darchen

At about 10:30 pm, the author reached Darchen. The author had a troubled night. He was suffering from cold and breathlessness. He tried to breath from his mouth. After a little while, he started breathing with single nostril. But the moment he dozed off, he woke up abruptly. His chest felt heavy. He sat up, which eased the pressure from his chest. When he tried to lie down and started dozing, he again felt uncomfortable.

Tsetan takes the author to the doctor

Tsetan took the author to Darchen's Medical College, which seemed new and looked like a monastery. In the consulting room, they found the doctor in a thick pullover and a woolly coat. After examining him, the doctor diagnosed it as cold and provided him, with fifteen screws of paper, which contained five day course of Tibetan medicine. The first packet contained a powder that tasted like cinnamon. The other contained brown pellets. To the author, they looked like sheep dung. After a full day's course, the author felt better and slept peacefully.

Darchen did not look so horrible to the author

After a good night's sleep, the author started enjoying Darchen. Once he felt better, Tsetan left for Lhasa. Darchen had a couple of small shops, which provided the basics for day-to-day use. The weather had improved.

The author's disappointment and his meeting with Norbu

The author was told that, at the height of pilgrimage season, the town gets a lot of visitors. But, probably the author timed his arrival a little early. There were not many people and none with whom the author could interact. As such, it hadn't been easy so far with all the difficulties that the author had faced. He did not want to do 'Kora' alone.

Though, the pilgrimage trail was much walked but the author did not feel comfortable doing it by himself. He was weary of the dirty ice that still clung to the banks of Darchen's brook. Then, the author met Norbu in a small cafe. The cafe had a single window and the author was sitting up close to it. When Norbu came to him probably, he had seen the note-book and a novel, which the author was carrying. Norbu asked him if he was an English man.

After ordering tea, they started talking. Norbu told him that he was a Tibetan but worked in Beijing. He had also come to do Kora. The author was extremely delighted because Norbu told him that he had been writing academic papers about the Kailash Kora but had never done it. Though the author was relieved to meet Norbu, his relief was short lived because he realised that Norbu was as ill-equipped as he was for the pilgrimage. Norbu was also very fat.

However, the author felt that Norbu would turn out to be a good companion. He wanted to hire some yaks to carry his luggage. He could not possibly climb because his tummy was too big.

Exercises

Notice these expressions

Question 1. "ducking back"

Answer   It refers to quickly going inside.

Question 2. "manoeuvres"

Answer   It refers to exercises involving a large number of animals.

Question 3. "billowed"

Answer   It refers to swelled out and went.

Question 4. "swathe"

Answer   It refers to long strip.

Question 5. "cairn of rocks"

Answer   It refers to pile of stones marking a special place.

Question 6. "careered down"

Answer   It refers to descended.

Question 7. "salt flats"

Answer   It refers to areas of flat land covered with a layer of salt.

Understanding the text

Question 1. Give reasons for the following.

(i) The article has been titled 'Silk Road'.

Answer   All along the route from Ravu to Mansarovar, the places that the author saw were festooned with white silk scarves and prayer flags. Also, Hor, was situated on the main East-West highway. It was the old trade route from Lhasa to Kashmir. Silk was one of the main export items. Hence, it came to be known as 'Silk Road'.

Question 2. Tibetan Mastiffs were popular in China's imperial courts.

Answer   Tibetan Mastiffs were huge black dogs that guarded the tents of the nomads. They were shaggy monsters who would speed directly to the target like a bullet from a gun. Their bark was ferocious and they were completely fearless. They used to chase away invaders. Their ferociousness made them popular in China's imperial courts as hunting dogs. They were brought along 'Silk Road' in ancient times as a tribute from Tibet.

Question 3. The author's experience at Hor was in stark contrast to earlier accounts of the place.

Answer   Previous travellers Ekai Kawaguchi, a Japanese monk, Sven Hadin, a Swede, were so moved by the sanctity of the lake that they had a sentimental outburst. But the author found Hor, which was situated on the shore of lake Mansarovar a grim and miserable place. There was no vegetation whatsoever, just dust and rocks liberally scattered with years of accumulated refuse.

Question 4. The author was disappointed with Darchen.

Answer Darchen was partially derelict and punctuated by heaps of rubble and refuse. The author was disappointed because it was not the tourist season and there were no pilgrims.

Question 5. The author thought that his positive thinking strategy worked well after all.

Answer The author was not willing to do the Kora all by himself. When he met Norbu and the latter told him his purpose to come to Mansarovar, the author was delighted. Norbu told him that both of them could be a team to do the Kora. This made the author think that his positive thinking strategy had worked.

Briefly comment on

Question 1. The purpose of the author's journey to Mount Kailash.

Answer The purpose of the author's journey to Mount Kailash was to complete the Kora, which was a sacred religious ritual according to Hindu and Buddhist tradition.

Question 2. The author's physical condition in Darchen.

Answer The author suffered a cold, which made him very uncomfortable. He had problems in breathing, especially when lying down. He felt that if he went to sleep, he would never wake up.

Question 3. The author's meeting with Norbu.

Answer The author was sitting in a cafe in Darchen when he met Norbu. He was delighted to meet him since Norbu was also planning to do Kora. Norbu, who worked in Beijing at the Chlinese Academy of Social Sciences, had written papers on Kailash Kora.

Question 4. Tsetan's support to the author during the journey.

Answer Tsetan was driving the vehicle for the author. He was a very efficient driver and managed to drive the tough terrains without any mishaps. Further in Darchen, when the author felt terribly sick, he tended well and took him to the doctor whose medicines cured the author.

Question 5. "As a Buddhist, he told me, he knew that it didn't really matter if I passed away, but he thought it would be bad for business."

Answer These were Tsetan's words spoken to the author. After the author's sickness was cured, Tsetan wanted to go to Lhasa. By saying these words, he showed his caring attitude towards the author and at the same time, he firmly reinstated that he was a Buddhist, who believed that physical death was not death in the real sense. However, he thought that the death of a tourist could affect his business as a taxi driver, badly.

Talking about the text

Discuss in groups of four

Question 1. The sensitive behaviour of hill folk.

Answer People in the hilly regions lead a very tough life. Everyday, they encounter death in one form or the other. This kind of experience makes them understand the value of life and this makes them sensitive to other people's needs as well.

People in the hilly areas have to face the travails of life. Also, basic supplies are in short supply in hilly areas. Thus, they learn to share and help. This trait is so evidently seen in Tsetan's behaviour. He is a skilled driver and knows the terrains completely. With his efficient driving, he makes author's journey quite hazardless. Even though Tsetan's job was over when they reached Darchen, he did not leave the author who had fallen sick. He looked after him well and left only when the author was cured.

Question 2. The reasons why people willingly undergo the travails of difficult journey.

Answer Human beings are different from other species because their sense of discerning is superior than the rest. But human minds are very strange. Most of us like to lead a very straight forward life, yet some of us always have the urge to do something different. This is the reason, few of us want to undertake adventurous tasks. Adventurous sports and adventurous journey are taken by these kind of people who are not only courageous, brave and daring but want to do something extraordinary.

The difficulties make the adventure more challenging. Some of us do not feel burdened or apprehensive when faced with problems. A glaring example is the author of 'Silk Road'. It is very difficult to complete the Kora of Mansarovar. He faces a lot of hazards on his way. To drive on a slippery terrain is not an easy task but the author's driver Tsetan does not flinch. However, the credit should be given more to the author as he is not the native of Tibet. He is not used to the severe climate nor is he accustomed to travel slippery hilly regions. It is his sense of adventure that surges him ahead to accomplish his task.

Question 3. The accounts of exotic places in legends and the reality.

Answer The world is full of places, which are very beautiful and exotic. We cannot visit all of them but we certainly like to read about them. The places of religious importance top this list of the places which we like to visit. Our legends about these places give such detailed exotic account that at the first opportunity we would like to visit them with a lot of expectation.

Unfortunately, these places bear the brunt of neglect. We realise it only when we go there. Whether it is Rameshwaram or Ayodhya or even Jagnnathpuri. The overall conditions of these places present a stark contrast from the account that we read. We get motivated to visit the places if we read about them or someone describes them.

However, when we actually see them, we realise that fiction is different from facts. The author of the lesson 'Silk Road' went to Mansarovar with a lot of expectations. He had read how the Mansarovar lake had an overwhelming effect on a Japanese monk Ekai Kawaguchi, and Swede, Sven Hadin. But when he visited Hor, a town sat on the shore of Mansarovar lake, he was aghast to see that Hor was a grim and miserable place with no vegetation, just dust and rocks liberally scattered with years of accumulated refuse.

Thinking about language

Question 1. Notice the kind of English Tsetan uses while talking to the author. How do you think he picked it up?

Answer He must have picked up English through his interactions with tourists.

Question 2. What do the following utterances indicate?

(i) "I told her, through Daniel ..."

Answer She was not able to follow English but Daniel translated what he told in English into the Tibetan language for her.

(ii) "It's a cold," he said finally through Tsetan.

Answer The doctor spoke in Tibetan language, which Tsetan translated into English for the author.

Question 3. Guess the meaning of the following words. In which language are these words found?

| kora   drokba   kyang |

Answer   *Kora* means pilgrimage.
Drokba means nomads.
Kyang means wild ass.
These words are found in the Tibetan language.

Working with words

Question 1. The narrative has many phrases to describe the scenic beauty of the mountainside like:
A flawless half-moon floated in a perfect blue sky.
Scan the text to locate other such picturesque phrases.

Answer

(i) .... the river was wide and mostly clogged with ice, brilliant white and glinting in the sunshine.

(ii) It was marked by a large cairn of rocks festooned with silk scarves and ragged prayer flags.

Question 2. Explain the use of the adjectives in the following phrases.

(i) shaggy monsters

(ii) brackish lakes

(iii) rickety table

(iv) hairpin bend

(v) rudimentary general stores

Answer

(i) Shaggy means hairy and unkempt.

(ii) Brackish means slightly salty.

(iii) Rickety means wobbly or shaky.

(iv) Hairpin means very sharp; shaped like a hairpin.

(v) Rudimentary means simple or basic.

Noticing form

Question 1. The account has only a few passive voice sentences. Locate them. In what way does the use of active voice contribute to the style of the narrative?

Answer   Some passive voice sentences are

1 The slope was steep and studded with major rocks...
2 It was marked by a large cairn of rocks.
3 The plateau is pockmarked with....

Passive voice is used only when the object is to be stressed. Passive voice is mainly used in reporting events. Active voice is more realistic and direct, thus contributing a more lively style to the narrative.

Question 2. Notice this construction: Tsetan was eager to have them fixed. Write five sentences with a similar structure.

Answer   The sentences are:

1 Savita was keen to get her cycle repaired.
2 Ravi was impatient to visit the exhibition.
3 Jagdish was itching to get started on his journey.
4 Malati was anxious to have her way in the argument.

1

A Photograph

Shirley Toulson

Central Idea

In the poem, the poetess is reminiscing about her dead mother. She sees her mother's childhood photograph and starts recollecting what the mother said. The mother is no more, but the poet could not help to realise that her mother's life was not a very happy one. The silence prevails.

Stanzawise Explanation of the Poem

The poetess looks at her mother's photograph

The poetess finds a photograph of her mother with her two cousins Betty and Dolly. The photograph was taken when her mother was twelve years old and had gone to the beach. Her mother, apparently, is older than both of her cousins. Each one was holding her mother's hand and and standing with the smiling face towards the camera. Her mother's face looked very sweet and the sea seemed to be washing their feet. They had gone for paddling.

Twenty-thirty years later

The poetess says that after a gap of almost twenty-thirty years, she sees her mother looking at the snapshot. The mother starts laughing, on seeing the photograph. She comments on how they were dressed for the beach. The poetess feels sad at the thought that the mother's laughter is a thing of the past. Probably, the time has robbed her mother of her happiness. It has been a long time since the poetess has seen her mother laughing.

The poetess' mother is dead now and only the photograph is left. The poetess is overwhelmed by the loss and tries to come to terms with her loss just the way her mother tried to bear the boys of laughter.

Exercises

Question 1. Infer the meanings of the following words from the context

Paddling   Transient

Now look up the dictionary to see if your inference is right.

Answer **Paddling**   wading in the water in bare feet

Transient   temporary

Dictionary Meanings

Paddling   walking through shallow water in bare feet

Transient   for only a short time

Think it out

Question 1. What does the word 'cardboard' denote in the poem? Why has this word been used?

Answer   The photograph is probably stuck on a cardboard. The mother is no longer alive. She is, now, as lifeless as the cardboard. The poetess has used work 'cardboard' to imply that the lively presence of her mother cannot be felt anymore. She is just a memory. The cardboard, also, is just a non-breathing piece, which reminds her of her mother who, once upon a time, was alive.

Question 2. What has the camera captured?

Answer   The camera has captured the three girls the poetess' mother and her two cousins who tried to stand to smile through their hair. They were at the beach.

Question 3. What has not changed over the years? Does this suggest something to you.

Answer   The sea has not changed over the years. It suggests that the prominent features of nature do not change much. Human beings come and go, but nature always remains.

Question 4. The poet's mother laughed at the snapshot. What did this laugh indicate.

Answer   The poetess' mother laughed looking at the snapshot because, suddenly, she was reminded of her happy and carefree childhood days.

Question 5. What is the meaning of the line, "Both wry with the laboured ease of loss".

Answer   The poetess is sad about the fact that her mother's laughter is history. Her mother feels the same for her childhood days. The word 'wry' here means disappointment. Both of them are disappointed and dejected over their loss.

Question 6. What does, 'this circumstance' refer to?

Answer   'This circumstance' refers to the death of the mother of the poetess. The happy and carefree girl seen in the photograph is no longer alive. The poetess could not help being sorry and sad to think of her mother a objected person. Who is no longer alive.

Question 7. The three stanzas depict three different phases. What are they?

Answer   The first stanza depicts the happy and carefree days of the poetess' mother when she was a young girl. That is her childhood. The second stanza depicts the middle age when the poetess' mother has forgotten to laugh because of the depressing circumstances.

The last stanza depicts a stage when the poetess mourn's the loss of her mother in a symbolic way. The mother's loss is not only a physical one but one of her identity, which leaves the poetess speechless.

2

The Laburnum Top

Ted Hughes

Central Idea

'The Laburnum Top' is written by 'Ted Hughes', the poet laurete of England. The silent laburnum tree comes to life with the chirrupings of the goldfinch bird. But, this liveliness lasts only till the time the goldfinch makes the tree abode. Once if it flies away, the laburnum comes back to its silent self.

Stanzawise Explanation of the Peom

The silent laburnum top

The top of the laburnum tree is silent and motionless. Its leaves are turning yellow and all its seeds have fallen down.

The goldfinch comes and the laburnum becomes lively

The sweet singing yellow goldfinch comes to the tree and the silent laburnum becomes full of life. Its arrival is sudden and the laburnum is vibrating with its chitterings, whisperings and trillings. It enters the thick tree and makes it tremble like a machine, which is in full force. The tree is like an engine to goldfinch's family. She comes there to overhaul it. She then shows her striped face, which is almost her mark of recognition.

The laburnum becomes silent again

The goldfinch starts chirruping in a strange but delicate voice and then flies into the infinite sky. After her departure, the laburnum is again left alone with its eerie silence.

Exercises

Find out

Question 1. What is a laburnum tree called in your language?

Answer   In Hindi, a laburnum tree is called the amaltaas tree.

Question 2. Which local bird is like the goldfinch?

Answer   The local bird similar to the goldfinch is the Indian Lutino Ringneck.

Think it out

Question 1. What do you notice about the beginning and the ending of the poem?

Answer   The first line of the poem is, "The laburnum top is silent, and the last line is, "And the laburnum subsides to empty". The entire activity of goldfinch is responsible for the laburnum tree to become vibrant. Goldfinch is not there in the beginning and flies away in the end, leaving laburnum silent, just the way it was in the beginning.

Question 2.   To what is the bird's movement compared? What is the basis for this comparison?

Answer   The bird's movement is compared to that of a lizard. Both are sleek, alert and abrupt. This is why, the comparison is very apt and convincing.

Question 3.   Why is the image of the engine evoked by the poet?

Answer   The engine produces a variety of sounds. It starts with a different sound and slowly changes to a different sound. The constant chirrupings and trillings of the goldfinch evoke the same effect.

Question 4.   What do you like the most about the poem?

Answer   I like the use of sound words and movement words the most in the poem. The abundance of sound words such as twitching, chirrupings, chitterings, trillings make the poem endearing to me. Similarly, movement words–fallen, a startlement, trembles, stokes–give the poem an entirely different shade.

Question 5. What does the phrase, 'her barred face identity mask' mean?

Answer The striped face of the goldfinch is its mask. She remains hidden in 'thickness' and her striped face makes her recognisable, and this face becomes her identity mark.

3

The Voice of the Rain

Walt Whitman

Central Idea

The poem, 'The Voice of the Rain' by 'Walt Whitman' is a celebration of rain, which takes the voice of a human being to answer the poet's question. The poem is a classic example of personification.

Stanzawise Explanation of the Poem

The poet's question and rain's answer

The poet asks the question to the falling shower about who it is. The poet was astonished to find the rain giving the answer. The voice of the rain says that it is the Poem of Earth. It is eternal and cannot be touched. It rises from the land and sea and goes upward towards the sky. There, it takes the form of the rain and sprinkles itself on the parched Earth and washes its dirt.

The Earth gets life from rain

Without rain, there would be no vegetation on the earth If there is no rain, there would be a severe draught. The rain is born from the Earth keeps its mother alive by pouring its contents, day in and day out. After the rain, the earth becomes pure and beautiful.

(The rain emanates from its birth place and after dispersing its duties, its goes back to its original place).

Exercises

Think it out

Question 1. There are two voices in the poem. Who do they belong to? Which lines indicate this?

Answer There are two voices in the poem. One belongs to the poet and the other one belongs to the rain. The line for the poet is, "And who art thou?" and the line for the rain is, "I am the Poem of Earth".

Question 2. What does the phrase "strange to tell" mean?

Answer We all believe that the nature has life, but we can never imagine that it has a voice also. That is the reason the poet was taken aback when the falling shower answered his question "strange to tell", hence, indicates the poet' surprise on listening to the voice of the rain.

Question 3. There is a parallel drawn between rain and music. Which words indicate this? Explain the similarity between the two.

Answer The similarity between rain and music is indicated by the words are 'soft falling' and 'song, issuing from its birth place'. The rain and musical notes fall softly on the Earth and ears respectively. The rain emerges from Earth and the song from its notes.

Question 4. How is the cyclic movement of rain brought out in the poem? Compare it with what you have learnt in Science.

Answer The cyclic movement of the rain is beautifully depicted by the poet. It rises out of the land and the sea in the form of the vapours. The atmosphere upwards cools it down and it falls in the form of rain on Earth. This is similar to what we have learnt about the water cycle in Science.

Question 5. Why are the last two lines put in the brackets?

Answer The last two lines are put in the brackets to give a more poignant and significant meaning to poem. The rain, like a song, after completing its course, comes back to its origin. It does not matter whether someone recognises its worth or not.

Question 6. List the pairs of opposites found in the poem.

Answer
    (a) Land and the bottomless sea
    (b) Day and night
    (c) Reck'd and unreck'd

4

Childhood

Markus Natten

Central Idea

The poet Markus Natten laments the loss of his childhood. The journey from childhood to adulthood is a gradual process. The poem passes through the three stages that a child undergoes

(1) Being rational
(2) Understanding hypocrisy
(3) Growing individuality.

Stanzawise Explanation of the Poem

The poet is disturbed about the loss of his childhood

The poet contemplates about the loss of his childhood. He wants to know the exact time, when he ceased to be a child. He wonders if it was the time, when he realised that heaven and hell are not physical places to be found in geography and, therefore, they are not real.

The poet understands the hypocrisy of adults' behaviour

The poet wonders, when the realisation that there is no similarity between what the adults say and what they do dawned upon him. They talk so much about love but they do not always act so lovingly. He keeps thinking, perhaps, that was the time, when he ceased to be a child.

The poet's rationality and maturity

The poet cannot help thinking when he exactly lost his childhood. There came a stage in his life; when he became rational and mature. He was able to think and take independent decisions. Perhaps, this was the time, when he lost his childhood.

The childhood can be found in an infant's face

The poet is obsessed with the loss of his childhood. He is sure that it has gone to a place, which everyone knows, but not one is able to retrieve it. The poet is sure that his lost childhood remains hidden on the innocent face of an infant.

Exercises

Think it out

Question 1. Identify the stanza that talks of each of the following.

individuality   rationalism   hypocrisy

Answer

    (a) individuality   stanza 3

    (b) rationalism   stanza 1

    (c) hypocrisy   stanza 2

Question 2. What according to the poem is involved in the process of growing up?

Answer According to the poem, the process of growing up has to pass through different stages. The first stage is when one starts differentiating between reality and imaginative realms. The second stage is the realisation of hypocratic behaviour of the adults. One comes to an understanding that there is a difference between what the adults preach and what they actually do. The last stage is the one of becoming independent and mature.

Question 3. What is the poet's feeling towards childhood?

Answer The poet, basically, seems to be obsessed about his childhood and, more so, about its loss. He feels very nostalgic and lament over the fact that his childhood will never come back.

Question 4. Which do you think are the most poetic lines? Why?

Answer   According to me, the most poetic lines are

Where did may childhood go?
It went to some forgotten place.
That's hidden in an infant's place.

These poignant lines explain beautifully what most of the adults feel. We all know that our pure and unadulterated childhood will never come back to us, though we know that it remains hidden on an infant's face.

5

Father to Son

Elizabeth Jennings

Central Idea

Elizabeth Jennings' poem 'Father to Son' is a very subjective poem. but seems to have a universal appeal. It deals with the general problem of 'generation gap'.

Stanzawise Explanation of the Poem

Father's dilemma of not understanding his son

The father and son are virtual strangers. The father feels that though they have lived together in the same house for years, he does not know his son at all. He wants to build a comfortable relationship with his son. He thinks about his son's childhood when, they were at ease with each other.

Father and son are strangers

Though the father is responsible to bring his son in this world, he has become an absolute strangers to him. They do not understand each other. The son's likes and dislikes are his own; the father does not get to know about it.

Father wishes his prodigal son's return

It is father's wishful thinking that his extravagant son should return back to the house, which he is familiar with. He does not want his son to move out of the house and make a world of his own. He is ready to compromise so that there can be a new beginning between them.

Both father and son want a closer relationship

The father and son live in the same world. They share the same planet yet what the son speaks, the father cannot understand and this makes him angry. The father is grieved, which is the result of his anger. Both, the son and the father want to come closer but do not know how to start. They want to forgive and forget.

Exercises

Think it out

Question 1. Does the poem talk of an exclusively personal experience or is it fairly universal?

Answer The poem is an autobiographical poem, but its appeal is fairly universal. What is portrayed in the poem, is a common occurence between any father and son. It is widely known as 'generation gap'. There is always a difference between the view points of father and son. They have a physical bond, but, mentally they drift apart. Both, the father and the son want to come closer but lack in understanding to initiate the move.

Question 2. How is the father's helplessness brought out in the poem?

Answer The father helplessness is brought out very poignantly in the poem. The father and the son do not talk to each other and, so, only silence prevails. The father does not want his son to be separated from him, but it is in vain.

Question 3. Identify the phrases and lines that indicate distance between father and son.

Answer   The following phrases and lines bring out the deep differences that separate both of them

1. I don't understand this child.
2. I know nothing of him.
3. We speak like strangers.
4. What he loves, I can't share.
5. Silence surrounds us.
6. He speaks, I can't understand.

Question 4.   Does the poem have a consistent rhyme?

Answer   Yes, the poem has a consistent rhyme scheme. Each stanza has six lines, which have the rhyme scheme-a, b, b, a, b, a.

1

The Summer of the Beautiful White Horse

William Saroyan

Chapter Sketch

This story is about two poor Armenian boys, who belong to a tribe whose trademarks are trust and honesty. The boys are tested for their honesty and they come out in flying colours.

The Story Retold

Mourad calls Aram to go for a horse ride

Aram recounts his experience when he was nine years old. At that age, the world appeared to be full of delightful and mysterious surprises. Mourad came to his house at about four in the morning and called him. When Aram saw through the window, he could not believe his eyes because Mourad was sitting on a beautiful white horse. Mourad invited him for a ride.

About their tribe

Aram was very fond of horses and had a longing to ride. Aram and his tribe were poverty stricken. They had been poor for generations. Nobody knew from where the money came to satiate their hunger. But, the most important characteristic of this tribe was that they were honest and their honesty had been famous for almost eleven centuries. So, it was very difficult to believe that Mourad could have stolen the horse.

Aram overcomes his hesitation to ride the horse

Aram knew that it was very difficult to believe that any person belonging to the Garoghlanian family (his tribe) could steal. He stared first at his cousin and then at the horse. When Mourad continously called Aram, he thought that probably stealing horse was not like stealing money. Probably, it was not stealing at all. After putting on some clothes, he jumped out of his window and joined Mourad on the horse's back.

The horse ride and Mourad's crazy streak

Aram and Mourad's house was at the edge of a town on Walnut Avenue. In a very short span of time, they reached another locality Olive Avenue. The author enjoyed the horse ride when suddenly Mourad started singing. To the author's ears, it was like a roar.

The crazy streak of the family

According to the author, every family had a crazy streak and his cousin Mourad was considered the direct inheritor of this characteristic. Before him, there was his uncle, Khosrove. He was a very big man with a large moustache. He had a furious temper and used to stop people by saying, "It is no harm, pay no attention to it". Once his son Ark covered a long distance to tell him that his house was on fire. Khosrove was in the barber's shop getting his moustache trimmed. Hearing the news, he got up from his chair and said, "It is no harm, pay no attention to it." Mourad was considered his natural inheritor.

Mourad wants to ride alone

After riding for a longtime, Mourad asked Aram to get down from the horse as he wanted to ride the horse alone. Aram asked Mourad whether he would also get to ride the horse alone. Mourad said that they would see because he knew everything about the horse.

After Mourad's ride, Aram also tries and the horse gets lost

Mourad, like a skilled rider, rode the horse across a field of grass to an irrigation ditch and five minutes later, returned. Then, it was Aram's turn. He leapt on to the back of the horse, but the horse did not move. Mourad got irritated and asked him to finish his ride because they had to return the horse.

The author kicked the horse and it began to run. But, instead of running across the field it ran down the road to the vineyard of Dikran Halabian, where it began leaping on vines. The author then fell from the horse but it kept running. Mourad came running and said that he was not worried about Aram but about the horse, who seemed to have been lost. It took half an hour for them to locate the horse.

They decide to hide the horse

Mourad was contemplating whether he should hide the horse or take him back to its owner. By his conversation, it became clear to Aram that Mourad had no intention of taking the horse to its owner. When he asked Mourad if he had stolen the horse, Mourad got offended. Aram then asked him how long ago he started riding. Mourad replied that it was only from that morning that he had started riding the horse. Mourad came out with the truth that it was indeed a stolen horse but if someone asked him he did not want Aram to be a liar so, he was not willing to tell him the entire truth. Mourad walked the horse to the barn of a deserted vineyard of a farmer named Fetuajian.

John Byro's visit to Aram's house

Aram and Mourad reached home after putting the horse into the barn. In the afternoon, Aram's uncle Khosrove came to his house. After sometime, a farmer named John Byro also arrived. He told them that his horse, which was stolen last month, was still missing. Uncle Khosrove started shouting, "It is no harm. What is the loss of a horse?" John Byro still complained which made Khosrove angrier. Byro felt really bad about his horse that costed him sixty dollars. Khosrove had no patience and walked out of the house.

Aram goes to Mourad

After the farmer left, Aram realised that Mourad had the horse for a month. He went to meet Mourad and told him that he knew that the horse was with him and he should keep it till the time Aram learnt to ride. Mourad says it would take an year for Aram to learn to ride. At last, Mourad agreed to keep the horse for six months.

Aram and Mourad meet John Byro

For two weeks, Aram and Mourad went for a ride with the same result. Whenever, Aram rode alone, the horse leapt over grapevines and threw him. One day on their way, they met John Byro. John Byro examined the horse eagerly. He asked them the name of the horse to which Mourad replied, "My heart", saw the horse closely. He told them had he not known the honesty of their family, he would have been sure that it was his horse. He felt that their horse was the twin of his horse.

The cousins take back the horse to its rightful owner

Next morning, they took back the horse to John Byro's vineyard. Mourad tied the horse, patted him and then both of them walked away. That afternoon, John Byro came to their house and told them that his horse had come back and was in a better state than what it was.

Exercises

Reading with insight

Question 1. You will probably agree that this story does not have breathless adventure and exciting action. Then, what in your opinion, makes it interesting?

Answer The story does not have breathless adventure and exciting action, but the element that makes it interesting is the smooth flow of psychological narration. Like any young boys, both Aram and Mourad, have their preference for something adventurous. They love horse-riding but the family cannot afford to have one. Mourad steals the horse and both of them enjoy the horse ride. But, their family is known for honesty and the same streak is present in them also. After a while, they overcome their greed and return the horse to its right owner.

Question 2. Did the boys return the horse because they were conscience stricken or because they were afraid?

Answer The boys returned the horse to Byro not because they were afraid but because their conscience pricked them.

When John Byro met the boys, the stolen horse was with them. John Byro recognised his horse but refused to believe that Mourad and Aram had stolen it. According to him, the fame of their honesty was widely known. This was the juncture when the conscience stricken boys decided to return the horse.

Question 3. "One day back there in the good old days when I was nine and the world was full of every imaginable kind of magnificence, and life was still a delightful and mysterious dream...". The story begins in a mood of nostalgia.Can you narrate some incident from your childhood that might make an interesting story?

Answer Reading these lines one cannot stop from travelling down the memory lanes of childhood. It was not long ago that my father was transferred to a place where there were not good schools. My parents were indecisive about taking me along or to leave me with my uncle. I insisted upon going with them. They were not left with any choice but to take me along with them.

'Raniganj' was a breathtakingly beautiful place. There was a huge palatial bungalow with a massive garden. Since it was close to the wild forests, I used to find a lot of wondering wild animals in my garden in the morning. What was very surprising was that none of them harmed me. One day, I saw a small deer. The moment I saw it, I decided to rear it. Everybody advised me against it. But, I had taken it as a challenge. Every morning, he would come sauntering down my garden. I used to feed him green leaves and water.

In two-three days time, we became good friends. Then, he would stay back in the Verandah at night. How the days flew! I started dreaming of keeping this beautiful creature always with me. Finally, my dream was shattered when after some time, my father was posted back to the city. I had to leave my beautiful friend in his natural habitat.

Question 4. The story revolves around characters who belong to a tribe in Armenia. Mourad and Aram are members of the Garoghlanian family. Now locate Armenia and Assyria on the Atlas and prepare a write-up on Garoghlanian tribes. You may write about people, their names, traits, geographical and economic features as suggested in the story.

Answer   **The Garoghlanian Tribe**

The Garoghlanian tribe is part of an Armenian community. Garoghlanian families were reputed for their honesty. They were once rich and prosperous and had their lands. But they had to flee their homeland due to war. As they had to flee from their homeland, they were living in abject poverty. They did not have enough money to buy food. But they maintained their moral values.

They were proud of their honesty. No member of a Garoghlanian family could be a thief. The people of this tribe were unique as they enjoyed 'being alive' despite their extreme poverty. Mourad expresses the desire to enjoy life when he steals the beautiful white horse to ride. Aram too had a keen desire to ride a horse.

Hospitality is also an important trait in Armenian culture. They entertained their guests with coffee and tobacco.

2

The Address

Marga Minco

Chapter Sketch

The story 'The Address', by 'Marga Minco' is a very touching account of a daughter, who goes in search of her mother's belongings, after the war in Holland. When she finds them, she is reminded of her earlier life, which disturbs her. She decides to leave them where they are and moves on in life.

The Story Retold

The author goes to Mrs Dorling

The author knocks at the door of a house. A woman opens the door and looks at her questioningly. The author asks her whether she knows her. The woman refuses to recognise her, even after the author mentions her mother's name. For a moment, the author thinks, perhaps, she has come to a wrong address and she does not know the woman. But at the same moment, the author gets a glimpse of the cardigan that the woman is wearing. Immediately, she recognises it as her mother's. She asks the woman if she knew her mother. The woman asks a very strange question, "Have you come back? I thought no one had come back". The author replies that only she has come back.

Mrs Dorling refuses entry to the narrator

On the narrator's enquiry, Mrs Dorling says that she cannot entertain her. She does not open the door of her house. She then tells her that it is not the convenient time for her to see the author.

The author goes back empty handed

After Mrs Dorling's refusal, the author walks back slowly to the station. She starts thinking about her mother. Her mother had given her the address of Mrs Dorling. The author goes down the memory lane. It was during the first half of the war that the author was at home and she, suddenly noticed that various things were missing from the home.

The mother's explanation

The author tried to inquire about it from her mother. Her mother replied that Mrs Dorling, whom she had not seen for years, had suddenly renewed their acquaintance. Everytime, she came, she took valuable things from the home.

Dorling took things from their home in order to keep them safe. There was a war going on and, in case, the author's mother had to leave her house, Mrs Dorling promised to save certain things. The author was not convinced. Now, as she goes back to the station, she tries to remember Mrs Dorling as she saw her the last time when her mother was bidding Mrs Dorling bye. This was the time, when her mother told her the address "in Marconi Street, Number 46."

The earlier reluctance of the author to look for her mother's belongings

It took a long time for the author to come and look for her mother's things. Initially, after the liberation, the author was not interested because she did not have any interest in seeing the "stored stuff". But, gradually everything became more normal. One day, the author decided to go back to the address and look at her old possessions.

The author decides to go to the address again

The author tries to go again to the address in Marconi Street Number 46. When the author knocks at the door second time, a fifteen year old girl opens the door. On enquiry, the girl informs that her mother is out for some work. The author said to her that she would wait.

She sees all her things

As the author follows the girl, inside the house, she notices-Hanukkah candle holder, table cloth, boxes, cups and plates, silver spoons, cutlery everything that belonged to her mother. She remembers, that one day, her mother had asked her to polish the silver and when she asked which silver, the mother had replied, that it was the spoon, forks and knives. That was the first time, she realised that their cutlery was sliver. The author suddenly feels queasy and wants to go back.

The author resolves never to remember that address

The author decides never to remember the address. She feels that there is no point in remembering those things, which have been dislodged from their place.

They lose their value when placed in strange surroundings.

Exercises

Reading with insight

Question 1. 'Have you come back?' said the woman. 'I thought that no one had come back'. Does this statement give some clue about the story? If yes, what is it?

Answer Yes, the words of this statement made by Mrs Dorling to the narrator give us some clues about the story.

This statement shows how the war caused devastation in the lives of the people of Holland. Before the war started, the people knew that it may start anytime. Mrs Dorling used to visit Mrs S the narrator's mother frequently. Mrs Dorling used to exploit her fears and insecurity by taking away her possessions like crockery and other valuable items from the narrator's mother, assuring her that she would keep those things safe during the war.

Mrs S trusted her to take care of the valuables while the narrator was not convinced of Mrs Dorling's intentions. The narrator and her mother had left Holland to save their lives during the war, like most other people in the town. The narrator's mother died before the war ended. The narrator came back to Mrs Dorling's address in search of her family belongings.

Mrs Dorling was shocked and surprised to see the narrator standing at her door when she made the statement given above. Mrs Dorling's statement shows that she knew the narrator, although she refused to recognise her. In fact, she behaved rudely and in an unfriendly manner.

Question 2. The story is divided into pre-war and post-war times. What hardships do you think the girl underwent during these times?

Answer The hardships which the girl went through at the time of the war are contrasted by her thoughts of the current situation. Some hardships during the war were:

   (i) The bread available was black in colour, showing that it was of poor quality.

  (ii) They could not sleep for fear of being attacked by the Germans.

 (iii) The view from the window used to be very horrifying, probably showing the atrocities of the occupying troops.

Question 3. Why did the narrator of the story want to forget the address?

Answer Once the war was over, the narrator went to Mrs Dorling's address in search of her mother's belongings. But the woman pretended not to recognize her. Nor did she show any intention of returning the things which she had taken from the narrator's mother. The narrator was shocked to see the 'nice belongings' of her mother being used in Mrs Dorling's house. She felt nostalgic and decided that she would not try to take them back, as they reminded her about the horrors of the war.

Since their true owner was no longer in this world, the possessions had lost their meaning. She felt that it was better to forget the address of the uncharitable Mrs Dorling, which symbolised a tragic past.

Question 4. 'The Address' is a story of human predicament that follows war. Comment.

Answer War brings with it death and destruction. Marga Minco's short story "The Address" describes human predicament that follows war. War had caused an upheaval in the lives of the people of Holland, as they lost their lives and homes. Mrs S was also a victim of the war.

So when the narrator, Mrs S's daughter, went to Mrs Dorling's house to claim those articles with which her mother's precious memories were associated, Mrs Dorling was surprised to see the narrator at her door and even pretended not to recognise her. The narrator was shocked to see the 'nice belongings' of her mother lying in Mrs Dorling's house. She felt nostalgic and the things appeared to have lost their worth in the absence of their true owner. Therefore, she decided to leave those things and forget the address forever.

Thus the story presents the upheaval in the lives of the narrator and her mother caused by the war. The story shows how war brings a dehumanizing effect on human beings. It kills the finer feelings of love and sympathy. It makes persons cruel and selfish.

3

Ranga's Marriage

Masti Venkatesha Iyengar

Chapter Sketch

'Ranga's Marriage', written by 'Masti Venkatesha Iyenagar' is a humorous narration. It is set in the village of Hosahalli where the villagers celebrate the homecoming of Ranga and the narrator tries to get him settled by fixing his marriage.

The Story Retold

The village of Hosahalli

The village of Hosahalli, where the narrator stays, was the erstwhile Mysore state in South India. Shyama, the narrator, gives an account of the happenings of ten years ago. Those were the days when very few people knew English. The village accountant was the first one who had sent his son Ranga to Bengaluru for higher studies.

Ranga comes home

When Ranga comes to the village, the entire crowd rushes to see him. They all want to find about the changes that might have taken place in him. Ranga greets them with a smile. Everyone is relieved and joyed to see him as he seems to be following the rules of a ritualistic family. The narrator blesses him and tells him that he should get married soon.

Ranga has no plan to get married soon

On narrator's enquiry about his plans of getting married, Ranga says that there is no such plan. He thinks that one should get married only when one is ready for it, both mentally and physically. Ranga further states that he would like to get married to a girl who is mature and he does not believe in 'arranged marriages'. All this distresses the narrator.

The talented Ratna, Rama Rao's niece

Rama Rao's niece Ratna is a pretty, eleven years, old girl. She is a talented musician. According to the narrator, she is an ideal bride for Ranga.

The narrator hatches a plan

The narrator visits Rama Rao's house frequently. Ratna is very free with him. On one Friday, the narrator goes to Rama Rao's place. He sends for Ranga and asks Ratna to sing. Ranga is enchanted by the singing. He asks the narrator if she is married. To this, the narrator says that she got married last year. Ranga is extremely disappointed on hearing this and leaves.

Choosing a bride for Ranga

The process of choosing a bride for Ranga starts. The narrator and Ranga go to the astrologer, Shastri, to find if everything is alright for Ranga as far as his planets are concerned. The astrologer asks Ranga what is worrying him. After making a pretention of calculations, he says that a girl is worrying Ranga and the name of the girl could be either 'Ratna' or 'Kamla'.

Shastri well instructed by the narrator

Shastri, in fact, has been told by the narrator beforehand what to say to Ranga. He does as he is asked to do by the narrator. The narrator then asks Shastri if there is any chance of Ranga and Ratna getting united in marriage. Shastri affirms the same and it makes Ranga happy. The narrator then asks Ranga if Ratna is the girl of his choice. Ranga admits the truth. The narrator then informs Ranga that Ratna is not married as yet.

The time flies

The time passes very quickly. Ranga and Ratna get married. One day, the narrator is invited for dinner on the birthday of Ranga's son Shyama. The narrator is touched by the fact that the couple has named their son after the narrator, Shyama.

Exercises

Reading with insight

Question 1. Comment on the influence of English - the language and the way of life - on Indian life as reflected in the story. What is the narrator's attitude to English?

Answer The story 'Ranga's Marriage' is set in a village Hosahalli, which was in the erstwhile Mysore state. In those days, there were very few people in Hosahalli who knew English. Like today, even during those days, English occupied a very prominent place in the hearts and the minds of people. The village accountant mustered enough courage to send his son, Ranga, to Bengaluru for higher studies. When Ranga returned home, it became almost a festive occassion for the entire village.

People had a lot of respect for Ranga because he knew English, which was a very precious commodity, but very few people in the village knew English. Even a simple word in English like 'change' was not heard of. When Rama Rao's son uses this word, even the narrator could not understand. He had to ask Ranga the meaning of the word.

The author, in his narration, shows that he has a positive attitude towards English, but he also asserts that learning a foreign language or knowing it need not affect our tradition and culture. This is evident by the emphasis on Ranga wearing the sacred thread and doing 'namaskars' to the elders.

Question 2. Astrologer's perceptions are based more on hearsay and conjecture than what they learn from the study of the stars. Comment with reference to the story.

Answer In today's India and India of yesteryears, there is not much of a difference as far as the belief in astrology is concerned. People believed in astrologers then and now. What we do not understand is that no one can predict God's design. The astrologers like Shastri, themselves, do not really know the correct calculations of the planents, but they pretend to do so.

Most of these predictions are based upon the information supplied earlier by someone. In the story, 'Ranga's Marriage', the Shastri is very well tutored by the narrator in advance. He tells Ranga exactly the same thing what the narrator asks him. He pretends to do all the calculations and moves his lips but these are all pretentions.

Question 3. What kind of a person do you think the narrator is?

Answer According to the story, the narrator is a very simple and kind hearted person. He seems to have a lot of admiration for his village and knows the smallest tit-bits about his place.

The narrator seems to have a clever perception and is a good judge of people. He realises that Ranga is a good groom for Ratna. He, then wastes no time and does everything for their marriage to be solemnised. His efforts culminate in a happy ending, for which he earns a lot of respect. This is evident when Ratna and Ranga name their son after him.

Question 4. Indian society has moved a long way from the way the marriage is arranged in the story. Discuss.

Answer In the story 'Ranga's Marriage', the entire process of choosing a bride for Ranga is based upon the system, which was followed long back in our country. Now the scenario has changed completely. Rarely, marriages happen at a young age. People have become conscious about the fact that if the marriage has to last, a certain sense of maturity is required and this maturity can be obtained through education only. When the boys and the girls decide to get married, they always make a conscious decision.

Now-a-days in India, marriages take place after the girl and boy consent to do so. Sometimes, the parents and the society do not approve but the Indian law supports this decision. In the story, 'Ranga's Marriage', the initiative for Ranga and Ratna's wedding was taken by the narrator. However, these days, we see a lot of changes taking place as far as the marriage scenario is concerned in India.

4

Albert Einstein at School

Patrick Pringle

Chapter Sketch

The lesson 'Albert Einstein at School' is a satire on education system. The author, Patrick Pingle, describes a pathetic experience of Albert Einstein at school. Einstein never considered school education interesting and fruitful.

The Story Retold

Einstein's indifference towards history

In one of the history classes, Albert Einstein is asked by the teacher to cite the date when the French were defeated at Waterloo. Einstein says that he does not know nor is he bothered as he does not see any point in remembering dates. According to Einstein, ideas are more important than facts and figures. The teacher gets very irritated and scolds Einstein.

Slum-violence–an Irritance for Einstein

Albert doesn't like school nor does he like the small room where he stays. This room is on one of the slums of Munich. His landlady is very short-tempered and beats her children. Her husband drinks on every Saturday and beats her. Albert feels miserable when he sees children crying all the time. He shares his anguish with his friend Yuri.

Einstein's meeting with his cousin Elsa

Eienstein's cousin Elsa meets him and tries to counsel him. She tells him that if Einstein tries a bit he would be able to pass the examination because there are boys more stupid than him. Einstein feels helpless as he is not good at learning facts. He likes soothing music and Geology.

Einstein asks Yuri to help him get a medical certificate

Einstein wants to leave the school. He asks Yuri to help him get a medical certificate, which would prove that he is suffering from a nervous break down and it is difficult for him to continue the school. Yuri promises to do this with the help of his doctor friend Dr Ernest Weil but warns him to be frank with the doctor.

Maths teacher gives a wonderful testimonial

Einstein manages to get a medical certificate from Dr Ernest Weil. Einstein reveals his plans to the doctor. He tells him that he intends to go to Milan and hopes to get an admission in some Italian institute. Yuri advises him to get a reference from his Maths teacher. Mr Koch, Einstein's maths teacher understands his calibre very well and gives him an absolutely glowing testimonial.

The head teacher summons Einstein

Einstein wants to meet the head teacher but before he could go to his office, he is summoned by the head master. The master informs him that he should leave the school and if he leaves the school on his own accord, the question of expulsion will not be raised. The head teacher gives several reasons to Einstein for his decision. Albert has no regret leaving the school. He only wants to meet Yuri who is his only friend in the city.

Exercises

Reading with insight

Question 1. What do you understand of Einstein's nature from his conversation with his history teacher, his mathematics teacher and the head teacher?

Answer Albert Einstein was an intelligent student, who was dissatisfied with the school education as it was based on rote-learning. The dissatisfaction of the history teacher with Einstein was primarily because of the fact that Einstein did not believe in learning dates and for the teacher, education meant only learning the dates and years of events.

Einstein's maths teacher's assessment was very different. He realised that Einstein's intelligence was much superior to his contemporaries. That was the reason, he gave a glowing testimonial to Albert.

Einstein's meeting with his head teacher was in an extremely bad taste. He wanted Einstein to leave the school as he had become a nuisance to others. Albert was very angry. He restrained himself and showed his contempt by not closing the door as his head-teacher had asked him to do.

Question 2. The school system often curbs individual talents. Discuss.

Answer School should be a platform from where the students can hone their talents. However, it is unfortunate that our system has turned education into a demanding monster. Education received in the school may not be the true education. True education promotes free growth and all-round development. But, the school system interferes with such development. There are a lot of restrictions and formalities in the form of assessments and activities. They are very time consuming and dreary.

The modern education system does not leave any space for a child to nurture his/her individual talent. They are all burdened with rote-learning which is measured by grades. This kind of system is almost claustrophobic for individual talent and a hindrance to the holistic development of a child.

Question 3. How do you distinguish between information gathering and insight information?

Answer As depicted in the story, the school education system is more concerned about information gathering rather than making students proficient in insight information. The teachers by students to learn dates and sequences by heart. They do not encourage the observatory and inferential skills of students that are essential to sharpen their intelligence. Whereas, information gathering is only about collecting data, insight information is analysing the information and making sense of it.

5

Mother's Day

J B Priestley

Chapter Sketch

JB Priestley brings out the plight of a mother in the story, 'Mother's Day'. The mother who plays a pivotal role in the family is treated shabbily by her husband and children. One day, she decides to act tough and set her family right.

The Story Retold

Mrs Pearson and Mrs Fitzgerald

Mrs Pearson and Mrs Fitzgerald are good acquaintance. Their personalities, nature, voice everything is poles apart. Mrs Pearson is a nervous looking woman while Mrs Fitzgerald is very strong. Mrs Fitzgerald is a fortune teller and she has learnt this art from the East.

Mrs Fitzgerald advises Mrs Pearson

Mrs Pearson is dominated by her family. Mrs Fitzgerald advises her to be strong and put her foot down. She tells her that Mrs Pearson is not the servant but the mistress of the house. She should not allow people to take her for granted. But, Mrs Pearson is basically a timid person and finds it difficult to do what Mrs Fitzgerald is asking.

Mrs Fitzgerald finds a solution to the problem

Mrs Pearson is not able to muster enough courage, so Mrs Fitzgerald tells her that they would exchange their personalities. She takes Mrs Pearson's hand and starts muttering "Arshtatta dum Arshtatta", and the transformation of the personalities takes place. Mrs Pearson becomes bold and Mrs Fitzgerald becomes timid and weak.

Doris becomes the first target

Mrs Pearson's daughter, Doris, orders her mother all day out. As soon as she sees her mother, she asks her to iron her yellow shirt, which she wants to wear that night. Doris is not prepared for what happens next. The mother does not respond. Then, Doris asks for tea, which, also, is not ready. Doris gets angry and then Mrs Pearson gives her a good dressing gown. She tells her, in no uncertain terms, how she puts in more working hours than Doris without pay. She ridicules her daughter for having an idiot of a boy as her boy-friend. Doris is dumbfounded.

Cyril gets a dressing down

Mrs Pearson's son Cyril comes and asks the question, "Is tea ready?" 'No', comes the answer. Cyril gets another shock when he asks his mother if she has put his things out and gets a total indifferent response. Both son and daughter are shocked to see their mother smoking and drinking. They feel that their mother has gone off the track. However, Mrs Pearson is adamant. She declares that she wants a forty-hour week for all. She does not want to work any extra hour.

Mr George's Pearson's turn

Mr George Pearson is surprised to find his wife drinking. Mrs Pearson ridicules her husband and tells him how he is the butt of jokes in the club. She further warns him not to shout at her. She threatens slap his big, fat, silly face. George is crestfallen and goes out.

Mrs Pearson can't take it any more

Mrs Pearson (in the personality of Mrs Fitzgerald) feels very bad about the way her family members are being treated. She requests Mrs Fitzgerald for the personality change. Mrs Fitzgerald agrees but warns her not to be soft with her family. George, Doris and

Cyril make an entry. They are a little weary. Mrs Pearson smiles and tells them that they will have a nice family game of rummy. After that, children will get the supper ready, while she would talk to her husband. Doris hesitates but, finally, gives her consent.

Exercises

Reading with insight

Question 1. This play, written in the 1950s is a humorous and satirical depiction of the status of the mother in the family

  (i) What are the issue it raises?
  (ii) Do you think it caricatures these issues or do you think that the problems it raises are genuine? How does the play resolve the issues? Do you agree with the resolution?

Answer

  (i) The main issue that the play raises is that the lady of the house, who is just like an axis, is never given her due respect, especially, if she is a simple housewife. The family members take her for granted. She works like an unpaid servant.

  The second issue is that the mistress of the house should assert her position very firmly to the family members. She should be ready to put across her views with determination rather than surrender meekly.

  (ii) The issues raised in the play are genuine even though they have been treated with satire and humour. The problem that we come across in our life has been depicted in the chapter very sensitively. The lady of the house should be the master of the house and she should make sure that all the family members should give her respect and recognition that she deserves. The issue is convincingly resolved in the play. The transformation of the personalities is symbolic. The author is portraying the fact that sometimes one has to put one's foot down.

Question 2. If you were to write about these issues today what are some of the incidents, examples and problems that you would think of as relevant.

Answer   If I were to write about some of the relevant issues today I wan't have to go very far. The same incident happens in my house also. We are three brothers and sisters, all school going children. My father is working in the office. My mother gets up early in the morning to prepare 4 sets of breakfasts and tiffins. We take our time to get ready but if there is a delay even of 5 seconds on the part of my mother, we all bring the roof down.

The same ritual takes place in the evening as well. Mother gets up before all of us and goes to bed after everyone.

We had all taken her presence for granted. One day, my grandmother fell sick and mother had to go for two days. Without her, the entire house looked as if it is hit by a tornado. We all waited for her as if we were waiting for some miracle to happen. When, finally she came, we all heaved a sigh of relief and vowed never to take her lightly.

Question 3. Is drama a good medium for conveying a social message?

Answer There is a very old cliche "Seeing is believing". When we hear something, we retain quarter, when we read, we retain half, when we see, we remember in full. Drama, when enacted, plays a vital role in making the concepts clearer. This is the reason, 'Nukkar Nataks' have gained so much popularity. The cine-art and the TV shows are making their foot-prints on the sands of time, precisely for this reason. They are viewed by a large number of viewers and generally, these visuals take universally accepted themes. Hence, drama is a good medium for conveying messages.

6

The Ghat of the Only World

Amitav Ghosh

Chapter Sketch

'The Ghat of the Only World' is a tribute to Agha Shahid Ali by 'Amitav Ghosh'.

The Story Retold

Agha Shahid Ali talks about his death

On 25th April, 2001, Shahid spoke to the author about his approaching death. Shahid Ali suffered from cancer and was under the treatment for 14 months. He was still lucid and on his feet. The author tried to tell him that he would be alright but Shahid was not convinced and wanted the author to write something about him after his death. Shahid, diagnosed with malignant brain tumor, had moved to Brooklyn to be close to his sister. The narrator promised him to do whatever he can.

Shahid a poet

Shahid's powerful collection "The country without a post office" had made a long lasting impression on the author even before he had met him. Shahid was originally from Srinagar and had studied in Delhi. They had frinds in common but they got to know each other only in Brooklyn.

After several conversations on the phone, they met a couple of times in 1998 and 1999. They shared a lot of things, which they liked, such as 'Rogan Josh', 'Roshanara Begum' and 'Kishore Kumar'. Both of them were not cricket lovers and liked old Bombay films.

Shahid's vitality

Shahid was to undergo a surgery. His head was shaved and the tumor was visible. Shahid refused to go on wheel chair and preferred to walk on his feet. He asked the hospital orderly where he was from. He learnt that man was from Ecuador. Shahid told him that he always wanted to learn Spanish and read in Lorca.

Shahid's gregariousness

Shahid was full of life. His spacious apartment had enough room to host and entertain friends and parties happened almost every evening. There were always poets, students, writers and relatives surrounding him. Even when he became blind, he could smell the Rogan Josh and was able to say whether it was ready or not. He was passionate about Kashmiri food in pandit style.

James Merrill's influence on Shahid's poetry

James Merrill influenced Shahid's poetry to a great extent. In fact, he was the one, who changed the direction of Shahid's poetry. Shahid was very fond of Begum Akhtar also.

Shahid as a teacher

Shahid's students were very impressed by him. He was a brilliant teacher. He had a series of jobs at colleges and universities. He was appointed as a professor in 1999 at the University of Utah in Salt-Lake city.

The deterioration of the political situation in Kashmir had a powerful effect on Shahid

In 1989, Shahid was much pained by the situation in Kashmir. He wrote, "The Kashmir would soon be in literal flames". He was not a political poet but Kashmir became the main subject of his poem. He was secular by nature. In his childhood, he wanted to have a Hindu temple in his room. When he did not respond to his treatment of cancer, he wanted to go to Kashmir to die. However, could not return to his native land and was laid to rest in Northampton.

Exercises

Reading with insight

Question 1. What impressions of Shahid do you gather from the piece?

Answer   The author Amitav Ghosh's write up on Shahid reveals that the poet was a multi-faceted personality. Even the dreadful disease of cancer could not break his spirit. He was a fighter and never lost courage in the face of misfortune. He refused to take the help of the wheelchair while in hospital and preferred to walk on his feet. He was an extremely gifted teacher as well.

Shahid was a profound lover of good poetry, good music and good food. He, himself, was a good poet and always enjoyed the company of poets and writers. His wit and sense of humour were also unique. Basically, he was a secular man. The political situation and violence hurt him so much that his poem's central theme became 'Kashmir'. He was a gifted person, indeed.

Question 2.   How do Shahid and the writer react to the knowledge that Shahid is going to die?

Answer   Shahid spoke to the narrator about his approaching death for the first time on 25th April, 2001. After a long conversation, Shahid wished that the narrator should write something on him. The narrator tried to console him that he would be fine soon, but the poet seemed to have accepted his fate with dignified grace. The narrator, at last, agreed to the poet's request.

Shahid never lost courage when the tests revealed that he had malignant tumor. He bore all the discomfort with fortitude even when he was about to undergo the surgery. He remained a fighter and preferred to walk rather than sitting on a wheel chair. In his last moments, he was at peace with himself and talked about meeting his mother in the life after death.

Question 3. Look up the dictionary for the meaning of the word 'diaspora'. What do you understand of the Indian diaspora from this piece?

Answer   The dictionary meaning of 'diaspora' is "the movement of people from any nation or group away from their own country". The narration,'The Ghat of the Only World' describes many Indians living in the United States, away from their motherland. Shahid lived in Manhattan and later shifted to Brooklyn. His sister taught at the Pratt Institute. Amitav Ghosh lived a few block away.

Though the narrator and Shahid lived in United States they loved Rogan Josh, Begum Akhtar and Kishore Kumar. Shahid had a passionate love for Kashmir, so that he wanted to go back to Kashmir to die.

7

Birth

A J Cronin

Chapter Sketch

'Birth', by AJ cronin, describes the efforts of a young doctor to save the life of a still-born baby and his mother.

The Story Retold

Morgan meets Andrew

Doctor Andrew reaches home almost at midnight, where he finds Joe Morgan, the driller, waiting for him. His wife is expecting their first baby almost after 20 years of their marriage. Doctor, immediately, sets out with Joe. When he reaches Joe's house, he finds Joe's 70 years old mother and the midwife waiting by the bedside of Mrs Morgan.

A very demanding case

The case turns out to be very demanding. Andrew decides to wait. As the doctor waits, his mind fills up with confusing-thoughts. He thinks about all the marriages, which have been failures. He thinks about his girl friend Christine, whom he loves. After an hour, the struggle for the baby to be brought in the world, starts. At last, the child is born but he does not breathe.

The doctor's dilemma

The doctor is shocked to see the stillborn child. He glances down at mother and realises that she also needs his urgent attention. He gets his priority clear and gives the child to the nurse. He directs his efforts to save the mother, who is in a very bad shape. She is sinking slowly. The doctor administers an injection and slowly but gradually, the mother stabilises.

The efforts, to save the child

The doctor examines the child and finds his face ashen white, which only means lack of oxygen. The child's pulse also extremely slow. Half an hour of laborious efforts yield no result. Then, the doctor rubs the lifeless body of the child with a towel and thumps the baby's chest with both his hands. Suddenly, the small chest heaves. The doctor doubles his efforts and slowly, the skin of the baby changes colour and turns pink. Finally, the child cries. The doctor hands over the child to the nurse and goes to Morgan who waits with an expectant face. The doctor delivers the good news that everything is fine.

The doctor is himself relieved at having done something worthwhile.

Exercises

Reading with insight

Question 1. "I have done something; oh, God! I've done something real at last". Why does Andrew say this? What does it mean?

Answer Andrew is a doctor and the primary duty of the doctor is to save life. When he is faced with a dilemma, he does not lose his balance and does what he is expected to do. He saves the mother first and, by his Herculean efforts, saves a nearly dead, still born baby boy. What he performed was nothing short of miracle. Doctor's sense of satisfaction is truly justified.

Doctors are expected to do their duties as and when demanded Andrew came home at midnight. He, surely, would have been tired but responded to the duty call when Joe Morgan asked him to come to his place. Morgan's wife needed immediate help. Andrew performed his duties exceptionally well. That is why he says,"I have done something; oh God! I've done something real at last".

Question 2. There lies a great difference between textbook medicine and the world of a practising physician. Discuss.

Answer From time immemorial, we have been hearing that there is a lot of difference between theory and practice. This, indeed, is true. The theoretical information gathered from the book, sometime, does not provide solutions to all the problems. The medical textbook provides information about the treatment of various diseases but at times, the doctors face a dilemma which cannot be solved by any orthodox theory.

In the lesson 'Birth' or Andrews undergoes the same experience. When the mother and son both needed his attention, he had to make a decision. In this decision making, no medical textbook could have helped him. In this case, Dr Andrew acted instinctively. He first saved the mother and then the child. He treated the mother with the traditional treatment and the child with a mixture of traditional and intuitive treatment. The net-result of both was success.

Question 3. Do you know of any incident when someone has been brought back to life from the brink of death through medical help. Discuss medical procedures such as organ transplant and organ regeneration that are used to save human life.

Answer The progress in the field of medical science is astounding. Everyday, new medicines are invented for various diseases, which make yesteryears treatment outdated and redundant. In fact, people say that after five years, the surgical procedure would be so advanced that today's surgical instruments will be termed as 'Butchers instruments'.

Organ transplant is such a procedure, which speaks volumes about the radical advancement in medical science. This progress turned out to be a real boon in my friend's life. She suffered a renal failure. Inspite of mammoth efforts, a matching donor could not be found. There was an appeal made for the donor in all the leading dailies and television, and the miracle happened - 'A perfect match was found'. The doctors wasted no time and the kidney transplant took place. With God's grace, my friend is leading a healthy life. It happened almost fifteen years back'.

8

The Tale of Melon City

Vikram Seth

Chapter Sketch

'The Tale of Melon City' is taken from 'Mappings' by Vikram Seth. The king, in this poem, is 'just and placid' but he carries his notion of justice a bit too far.

The Story Retold

Just and placid king

The king wants an arch to be built, which would be a symbol of his triumphs. This arch should pass through the thoroughfare of the city to inspire and motivate the people. The workmen spare no efforts to do the king's bidding and then, the king rode down the thoroughfare to inspire others.

The king loses his crown and frowns

The constructed arch turns out to be very low. When the king approaches the arch and goes under it, his crown is banged and lost. The king gets angry and orders the chief of builders to be hanged. Arrangements are made for the hanging. The chief pleads that it is workmen's fault. The workmen say it is not their fault but the bricks used in the arch were of wrong size. Then, the masons are to be hanged. They shift the blame to the architect, who in turn, says that it is the king who altered the original plan of the arch, hence the problem.

The king needs counsel

The king realises that he is caught in a tricky situation. He wants the wisest man to find an answer to handle the situation. The wise man says that a thing that touched the royal head could not be hanged. The king agrees.

Crowd wants some action

The onlookers of this drama get restless. The king perceives the mood of the crowd and declares "the nation wants a hanging". A noose is set up at height and each man is measured. Only one man is found so tall that his neck could fit in the noose and he was the king himself. His majesty is, therefore,"hanged by the Royal Decree".

The nation now has to choose a new king

The ministers are now relieved that the hanging has taken place, otherwise, there would have been a revolt. Now, they have to choose another king. Since they are very practical (punintended), they decide that whoever is the first to pass the city gate would choose the king.

An idiot decides who should be the next king

The man who passes the city gate first is an idiot. He gives his choice - a 'melon' to be the next king.

The ministers take the melon with all the fanfare to the throne. This happened long-time back. When someone asked the people why they chose a melon to be their king, they replied that it was a customary choice. It made no difference if their king was a melon or a human being. They were happy, atleast, the melon king would not interfere in their lives. They would be free to live in peace and liberty.

Exercises

Reading with insight

Question 1. Narrate 'The Tale of Melon City' in your own word.

Answer The lawful and gentle king of a city once had a desire for building an arch across the main road to enlighten the people. Workmen constructed the arch as the king had ordered it. When the king rode down the main road and passed under the arch, his crown struck the arch and fell down. Furious at his disgrace, the king ordered the chief of builders to be hanged. But the chief of the builders blamed the workmen for the mistake. The workmen blamed the masons for making the bricks of the wrong size. The masons blamed the architect for making the wrong plans. The architect put the king in dilemma, as he reminded the king that he himself had made a change in the plans made by the architect.

The king wanted the wisest man in the city to decide the guilty person. An old man, who could neither see nor walk, was considered the wisest because of his age. He blamed the arch itself for the disgrace. But a Councillor said that something that touched the king's head should not be punished. Meanwhile, the people were getting restless and the king understood that guilty or not, somebody must be hanged.

So, he asked for the loop of rope to be used for the hanging to be set high and anyone whose head reached it would be hanged. One by one all the people were measured but nobody reached its height except the king himself, as he was the tallest. So, according to the royal order, the king himself was hanged. The ministers heaved a sigh of relief after hanging the king. But a new crisis arose: who would be the king? So, the ministers decided that the next man who passed the City Gate would choose the king.

An idiot who was fond of melons happened to pass the gate first. The guards asked him about who should be the king to which his answer was, 'a melon'. So, a melon was named the king and was crowned in a proper ceremony. The people were happy to have a melon as king as long as it left them in peace and at liberty.

Question 2. What impression would you form of a state where the king was 'just and placid'?

Answer The poem is a satire. It satirises how a 'just and placid' king rules the state and passes it on to a melon. The king lives in a world of his own. He lacks the will and the discretion to rule his kingdom. He is incapable of taking independent decisions.

This kind of whimsical and fickle minded king can bring the entire state to a halt. Everyone should be ready to meet the unexpected. When the low arch bangs the crown, the king gets angry and blames chief of the builders and sentences him to death. Then, the blame game starts. The king being a just and placid king keeps changing his decision till the onus falls on him and he is hanged. Ultimately, the king has to pay to a very heavy price for being just.

Question 3. How, according to you, can peace and liberty be maintained in a state?

Answer   Peace and liberty are the two strong factors for a state to flourish. The rules of the state should bc judicious and sensitive to the needs of its people. A strong ruler must be intelligent enough to make his people understand the difference between liberty and anarchy.

An intelligent and powerful king can bring peace and liberty in the real sense. Ironically, in the poem "The Tale of Melon City', the king is just and placid but the outcome was that the state passes on to a melon.

Question 4. Suggest a few instances in the poem which highlight humour and irony.

Answer   'The Tale of Melon City' is full of irony and humour. There is a 'just and placid' king who in the end, becomes the victim of his own sense of justice. He is 'placid' but flares up on small issues and passes death sentence.

The king, who is supposed to rule, gets ruled by others - chief of builders, masons, architect, wise man, and so on and so forth. After the death of the king, the state is ruled by a melon. It is humorous to the extent of being ridiculous. But underneath lies a message - when people are disillusioned and without direction, it hardly matters to them who their king is - a human being or a melon.

Ingram Content Group UK Ltd.
Milton Keynes UK
UKHW021400250423
420747UK00015B/624

9 789327 198089